Visual Reference

Microsoft®
Windows® 95

At a Glance

Microsoft Press

Microsoft Windows 95 At A Glance

PUBLISHED BY
Microsoft Press
A Division of Microsoft Corporation
One Microsoft Way
Redmond, Washington 98052-6399

Library of Congress Cataloging-in-Publication Data
Joyce, Jerry, 1950–

    Microsoft Windows 95 at a glance / Jerry Joyce and Marianne Moon.
      p.   cm.
    Includes index.
    ISBN 1-57231-370-6
    1. Microsoft Windows (Computer file).   2. Operating systems (Computers).
    I. Moon, Marianne.   II. Title.
    QA76.76.063J693   1997
    005.4'469—dc21   96-29986
                                         CIP

Printed and bound in the United States of America.

5 6 7 8 9 QEQE 2 0 1 9 8

Distributed to the book trade in Canada by Macmillan of Canada, a division of Canada
Publishing Corporation.

A CIP catalogue record for this book is available from the British Library.

Microsoft Press books are available through booksellers and distributors worldwide. For further
information about international editions, contact your local Microsoft Corporation office.
Or contact Microsoft Press International directly at fax (206) 936-7329.

Acquisitions Editor: Kim Fryer   **Technical Editor:** Michael T. Bunney
Project Editor: Lucinda Rowley   **Manuscript Editor:** Marianne Moon

Contents

Windows 95 is your working headquarters.

See page 6

Windows remembers where things belong.

See page 21

Find a folder or a file
See pages 30–33

"Look, Ma, I'm multitasking!"

See page 46

Meet Windows Explorer
See page 53

Create a picture
See page 68

Associate a sound
with an event
See page 84

Back up your work!

See pages 91–96

Work in MS-DOS
See pages 101–112

Clean up your Desktop!
See page 128

Change your mouse
pointer
See page 135

Add fonts
See page 160

Welcome to the
Network Neighborhood!
See page 165

11 Using Mail, Fax, and Phone 193

"How do I change my passwords?"

See page 190

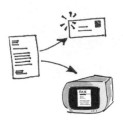

Reply to e-mail
See pages 200–201

Send faxes and e-mail from one message
See page 212

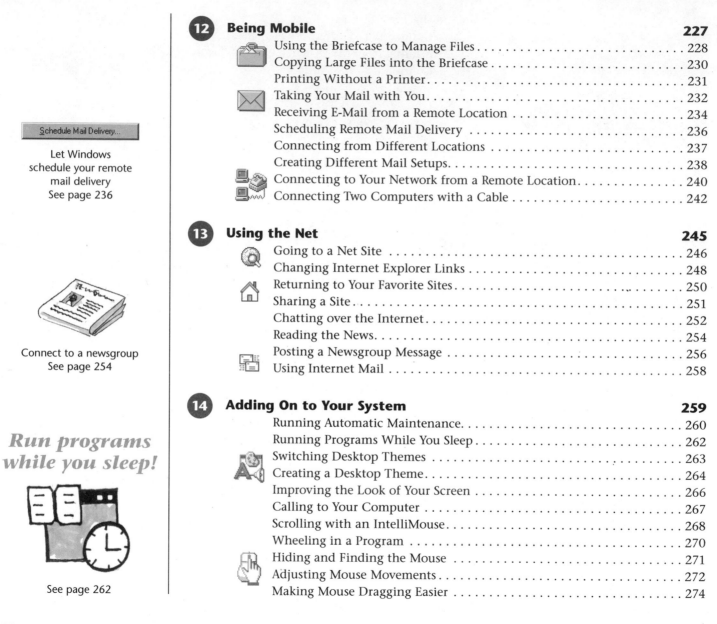

Schedule Mail Delivery...

Let Windows
schedule your remote
mail delivery
See page 236

Connect to a newsgroup
See page 254

*Run programs
while you sleep!*

See page 262

Acknowledgments

This book is the result of the combined efforts of people whose work we trust and admire and whose friendship we value highly. Ken Sanchez and Kari Becker, our talented typographers, meticulously laid out the complex design. Michael Bunney, our eagle-eyed technical editor, double-checked every procedure and every graphic to verify that things worked as described. Susan Bishop produced the interior graphics and the illustrations; we worked with Sue on the *Microsoft Publisher Companion,* and we're happy to have her distinctive drawings in our book. We've worked with Alice Copp Smith on other books. She does so much more than proofread: her gentle and humorous chiding teaches us to write better. And our indexer, Kari Bero, seems to inhale the soul of a book and magically exhale an extensive index. Thanks also to Herbert Payton for patiently answering lots of questions, and to Todd Emery and Paul Ampadu for their help with the graphics.

At Microsoft Press, first and foremost we thank Lucinda Rowley for making it possible for us to write this book. Thanks also to Judith Bloch, Kim Eggleston, Kim Fryer, Mary DeJong, Nancy Jacobs, Jim Kramer, and William Teel, all of whom provided help and valuable advice along the way.

On the home front, Roberta Moon-Krause and Rick Krause allowed their puppies, Baiser and Pierre, to roam freely on our virtual and literal desktops. Pierre decided not to appear in this book, but Baiser graces some of our pages with her furry little image. Roberta brought us many a wonderful home-cooked dinner as we toiled long into the night, and Rick helped with details too numerous to mention. Thanks, kids—you're the greatest!

About This Book

Microsoft *Windows 95 At A Glance* is for everyone who wants to get the most from their computer and their software with the least amount of time and effort. Whether you stood in line at midnight on August 24, 1995 so that you could be the first on your block to get a copy of Windows 95 or just bought a computer with Windows 95 preinstalled, you'll find this book to be a straightforward, easy-to-read reference tool. With the premise that your computer should work for you, not you for it, this book's purpose is to help you get your work done quickly and efficiently so that you can get away from the computer and live your life.

No Computerese!

Let's face it—when there's a task you don't know how to do but you need to get it done in a hurry, or when you're stuck in the middle of a task and can't figure out what to do next, there's nothing more frustrating than having to read page after page of technical background material. You want the information you need—nothing more, nothing less—and you want it now! *And* it should be easy to find and understand. That's what this book is all about. It's written in plain English—no technical jargon and no computerese. No single task in the book takes more than two pages. Just look up the task in the index or the table of contents, turn to the page, and there's the information, laid out step by step and accompanied by graphics that add visual clarity. You don't get bogged down by the whys and wherefores: just follow the steps, look at the illustrations, and get your work done with a minimum of hassle.

Occasionally you might have to turn to another page if the procedure you're working on has a "See Also" in the left column. That's because there's a lot of overlap among tasks, and we didn't want to keep repeating ourselves. We've also scattered some useful tips here and there, and thrown in a "Try This" once in a while, but by and large we've tried to remain true to the heart and soul of the book, which is that the information you need should be available to you at a glance.

Useful Tasks...

Whether you use Windows 95 for work, play, or some of each, we've tried to pack this book with procedures for everything we could think of that you might want to do, from the simplest tasks to some of the more esoteric ones.

...And the Easiest Way to Do Them

Another thing we've tried to do in *Windows 95 At A Glance* is to find and document the easiest way to accomplish a task. Windows often provides a multitude of methods to accomplish a single result, which can be daunting or delightful, depending on the way you like to work. If you tend to stick with one favorite and familiar approach, we think the methods described in this book are the way to go. If you like trying out alternative techniques, go ahead! The intuitiveness of Windows invites exploration, and you're likely to discover ways of doing things that you think are easier or that you like better than ours. If you do, that's great! It's exactly what the creators of Windows 95 had in mind when they provided so many alternatives.

A Quick Overview

This book isn't meant to be read in any particular order. It's designed so that you can jump in, get the information you need, and then close the book and keep it near your computer until the next time you need to know how to get something done. But that doesn't mean we scattered the information about with wild abandon. If you were to read the book from front to back, you'd find a logical progression from the simple tasks to the more complex ones. Here's a quick overview.

First, because so many computers come with Windows 95 preinstalled, we assume that Windows 95 is already installed on your machine. If it's not, the Setup Wizard makes installation so simple that you won't need our help anyway. So, unlike many computer books, this one doesn't start out with installation instructions and a list of system requirements. You've already got that under control.

Sections 2 through 5 of the book cover the basics: starting Windows; starting programs; using shortcut menus; creating, finding, and organizing files and folders; and working with the programs that come with Windows 95, including multimedia.

Sections 6 through 9 describe tasks that are a bit more technical but are really useful: backing up information, creating additional disk space, customizing just about every part of Windows 95 so that it looks and works the way you want it to, and adding and removing software and hardware components. If you think these tasks sound complex, rest assured that they're not; Windows 95 makes them so easy that you'll sail right through them. There's also a small section here for faithful fans of MS-DOS.

Sections 10 through 15 are all about communicating with your coworkers and using Windows 95 as your window on the world at large: working in a workgroup, communicating electronically using e-mail and fax, doing your work in a different location (yes, at the beach if you like), and expanding your horizons with the Internet and/or a company intranet.

A Final Word (or Two)

We had three goals in writing this book, and here they are.

◆ Whatever you *want* to do, we want the book to help you get it done.

◆ We want the book to help you discover how to do things you *didn't* know you wanted to do.

◆ And if we've achieved the first two goals, we'll be well on the way to the third: we want the book to help you *enjoy* doing your work with Windows 95. We think that would be the best gift we could give you as a "thank-you" for buying our book.

We hope you'll have as much fun using this book as we've had writing it. The best way to learn is by *doing*, and that's how we hope you'll use *Windows 95 At A Glance*.

Jump right in!

2

Jump
Right In

Microsoft Windows 95 is designed to work for you, not you for it. Don't be afraid to jump right in, look around, and try out some features. You'll find that there are often several ways to accomplish one task. Why? Because people work differently. Because different tasks have different requirements. And so that you can find the way that works best for you, get your work done quickly, and get away from the computer!

You'll find that most of the procedures are simple and straightforward and that Windows often uses automated methods to help you get the more complex chores done easily. This doesn't mean that you can't get stuck or get into trouble, but there are so many safeguards built into Windows 95 and so many places to get help that you'll have to work pretty hard to get into *real* trouble.

This section of the book covers the really basic stuff, from starting up Windows 95 through shutting it down. There's also a handy visual glossary on the following two pages that will help you become familiar with the names of the various parts of the Windows 95 environment.

Don't change or delete anything just yet, though—you want to feel comfortable with the basics before you do any customizing. The best way to learn about running programs, managing windows, and getting help if you *do* get into trouble is to jump right in and try it.

Windows at a Glance

Windows 95 is your working headquarters—the *operating system* that makes it possible for you to run different programs simultaneously and share information between programs if you need to. Most of the programs you'll use have common characteristics that were designed to work together in the Windows environment—meaning that once you learn how to do something in one program, you know how to do it in other programs.

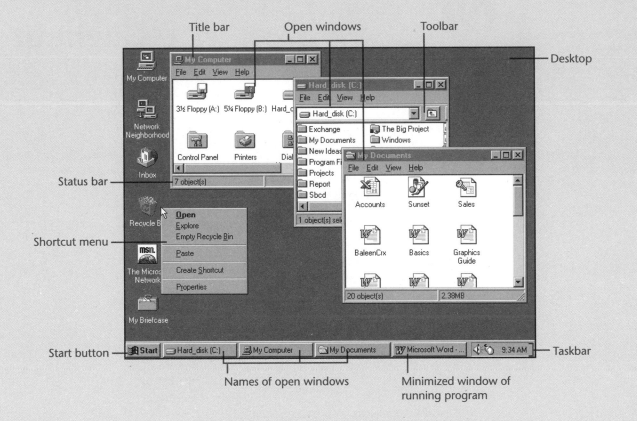

Take a look at the different parts of the Windows environment that are displayed on these two pages—what they do and what they're called—and you'll be on the road to complete mastery! Windows 95 is so intuitive that you'll learn by doing, but you can always come back to this visual glossary for a quick refresher on Windows terminology.

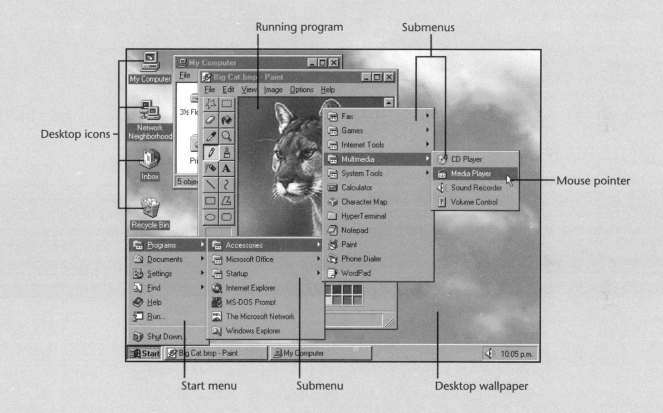

Running program

Submenus

Desktop icons

Mouse pointer

Start menu

Submenu

Desktop wallpaper

Starting Up

When you turn on your computer, you're also starting Windows 95. When Windows 95 starts, it loads programs and files into the computer's memory. The time your computer takes to start up depends on its speed and configuration (including network connections) and on the programs that are set up to start when Windows starts. Depending on the configuration, you might never be asked for a password, or you might be asked for a password twice—once to log on to Windows and once to log on to your network.

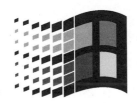

Start Windows

1 Turn on your monitor.

2 Turn on your computer.

3 Turn on any peripheral devices—your printer, for example.

4 Wait. A graphical meter at the bottom of the screen shows, sometimes in a rather convulsive manner, that Windows 95 is continuing to load.

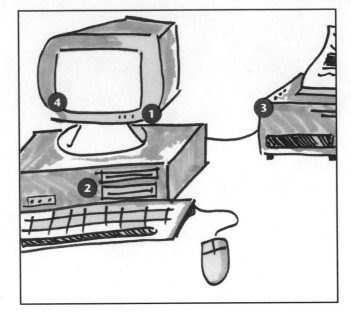

Enter Your Password

1. Type the name you've been assigned in the User Name text box if it's not already there, and press the Tab key.

2. Type your password in the Password text box. For a network logon, be sure to use the correct capitalization!

3. If you're logging on to a LAN, the domain name will probably be filled in for you already. If not, press Tab again and type the network domain name in the Domain text box.

4. Click OK.

Windows logon

Network logon

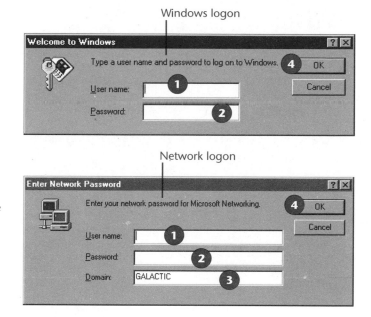

Starting a Program

Despite all the hype, the real work of an operating system is to run your software programs. Windows usually gives you several different ways to start up your programs, so you can choose the way that's easiest for you or that you like the best.

SEE ALSO

"Mouse Maneuvers" on page 14 for detailed information about pointing, clicking, and double-clicking with a mouse.

"Placing Shortcuts on the Desktop" on page 122 for more information about accessing programs from the Windows Desktop.

Start a Program from the Start Menu

1. Click the Start button.

2. Point to the Programs menu item.

3. Continue pointing to groups as the submenus cascade out. If you don't see the program you want, point to a group where it might be located.

4. When you see the program you want, point to it and click to choose it.

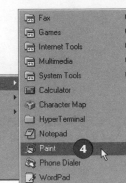

Start a Program from the Desktop

Point to the program icon and double-click.

TIP

Start a Program from a CD. *Many CDs have a feature called AutoPlay—you simply insert the CD into the CD-ROM drive and Windows starts the program automatically. If you want to grab some files from the CD without starting the program, hold down the Shift key while inserting the CD.*

SEE ALSO

"Exploring Windows with Windows Explorer" on page 54 if you want to try another way of navigating through your drives and folders to start programs.

Start a Program from My Computer

1 Double-click the My Computer icon.

2 Double-click the drive that contains the program you want to start.

3 Double-click the folder that contains the program. If the program is in a subfolder, continue double-clicking the subfolders until you reach the program you want.

4 Double-click the program icon.

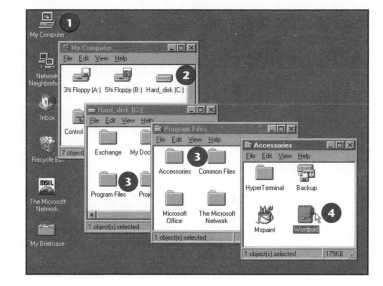

Managing a Program Window

"Managing" a window means that you can boss it around: you can move it, change its size, and open and close it. Most programs are contained in windows. Although these windows might have some different features, most program windows have more similarities than differences.

SEE ALSO

"Mouse Maneuvers" on page 14 for information about dragging and dropping.

Move a Window

1. Point to the title bar.

2. Drag the window and drop it at a new location.

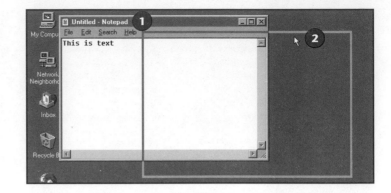

Use the Buttons to Switch Between Sizes

1. Click the Maximize button, and the window enlarges and fills the screen. (If the window is already maximized, you won't see the Maximize button.)

2. Click the Restore button, and the window gets smaller. (If the window is already restored, you won't see the Restore button.)

3. Click the Minimize button, and the window disappears but you see its name on a button on the taskbar.

4. Click the window's name on the taskbar, and the window zooms back to the size it was before you minimized it.

Program title bar   Buttons for switching between window sizes

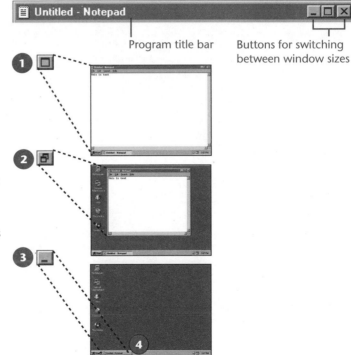

SEE ALSO

"Managing Multiple Programs" on page 46 for information about automatically arranging all your program windows.

TIP

Save, Save, Save! *Don't wait until you quit a program to save your work. You never know what disaster is about to befall you, so be cautious and save your work frequently.*

TIP

Move Your Mouse...*over a side border to change the window's width; over a top or bottom border to change the window's height; over a corner to change both height and width.*

Use the Mouse to Resize a Window

1. Click the Restore button if the window is currently maximized. (You can't manually size a maximized window.)

2. Move the mouse over one of the borders of the window until the mouse pointer changes into a two-headed arrow. The directions of the arrowheads show you the directions in which you can move the window border.

3. Drag the window border and drop it when the window is the size you want.

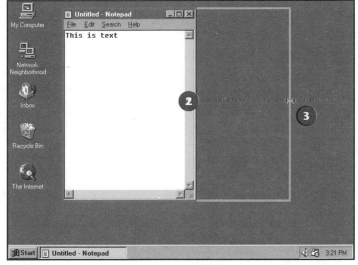

Close a Window

1. Click the Close button.

2. If there's work that you haven't yet saved, the program asks you whether you want to save it. Click Yes to save it, No to discard it, or Cancel if you've changed your mind about closing both the window and the program.

Mouse Maneuvers

Navigating with a mouse is like traveling in a helicopter: you can lift off from any spot, fly a straight line over hills and canyons, and set down wherever you want. Using the keyboard to navigate is like taking the scenic route: you'll run into detours in a program's topography, and you might need a good map to navigate through menus and shortcut keys to reach your destination. You might prefer the longer keyboard route—you get to explore the road less traveled, and you might even come across features and techniques that are new to you. But to finish your tasks as quickly as possible—and to take advantage of some of Windows' best features—give your mouse the job!

Before you fly off on your mouse wings, though, you might need some Mouse Basics. At Mouse School, we believe there are no bad mice (okay, mouse devices)—only bad mouse operators. Here you'll learn to point, click, double-click, right-click, select, and drag and drop.

Point: Move the mouse until the mouse pointer (the small arrow-shaped pointer on the screen) is pointing to the item you want.

Click: Point to the item you want, and then quickly press down and release the left mouse button.

Double-click: Point to the item you want, and then quickly press down and release the left mouse button twice, making sure that you don't move the mouse between clicks.

Right-click: Point to the item you want, and then quickly press down and release the right mouse button.

Select: Click the item you want. A selected item is usually a different color from other similar items, or is surrounded by a frame.

Drag and drop: Select the item you want. Then, keeping the mouse pointer on the selected item, hold down the left mouse button, move the mouse until the item is at the desired location, and then release the left mouse button to "drop" the item.

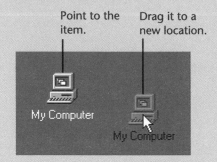

Point to the item.

Drag it to a new location.

My Computer

My Computer

You can customize the way your mouse works, including switching the roles of the left and right mouse buttons (but you'll have to remember to reverse left and right in the previous instructions). For more information on customizing your mouse settings, see "Customizing Mouse Operations" on page 138. If you have an IntelliMouse, you'll want to read pages 268–274.

Using Shortcut Menus for Quick Results

Windows 95 and the programs that work with it were designed to be intuitive—that is, they anticipate what you're likely to want to do when you're working on a particular task, and they place the appropriate commands on a shortcut menu that you open by clicking the *right* mouse button. These shortcut menus are *dynamic,* which means that they change depending on the task in progress.

TIP

If in Doubt, Right-Click.
If you're not sure how to accomplish something, right-click, and you'll often see the appropriate command on the shortcut menu.

Use a Shortcut Menu Command

1 Right-click an item.

2 Choose a command from the shortcut menu to accomplish the task at hand. (A few items and the shortcut menus they produce when right-clicked are shown here.)

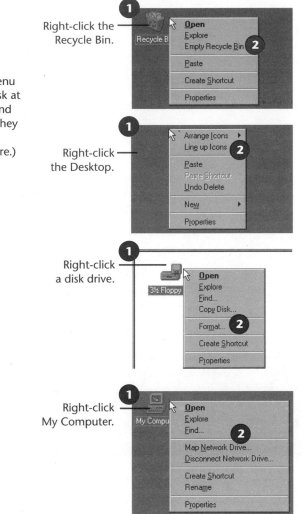

Right-click the Recycle Bin.

Right-click the Desktop.

Right-click a disk drive.

Right-click My Computer.

Getting Help

What's big and colorful; packed with information, procedures, tools, and videos; and sadly under-utilized? The Help programs! Of course, they couldn't possibly replace this book, but you can use them to find concise step-by-step procedures to diagnose and overcome problems, see demonstrations on how to work in Windows, and learn how to accomplish your tasks faster and more easily than you ever imagined.

Read a Procedure from Windows Help

1 Click the Start button, and choose Help.

2 Click the Index tab.

3 Type a word that describes what you want to do.

4 Double-click the related word or phrase in the list box.

5 Read the topic.

6 Click the Help Topics button to see more topics.

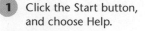

Help Topics: Windows Help

Contents | Index | Find

1 Type the first few letters of the word you're looking for.

help

2 Click the index entry you want, and then click Display

> when you press keys
> **Help**
> adding bookmarks to Help topics
> adding comments to Help topics
> color of Help window, changing
> copying information from
> Find tab, using
> finding similar topics in
> finding topics in
> finding words or phrases in
> font size in Help window, changing
> getting Help in dialog boxes
> going back to previous topics
> keeping Help in front of other windows
> MS-DOS command help
> printing a copy of Help information
> tips for using

Display

Windows Help

Help Topics | Back | Options

To find a topic in Help

1 Click the Contents tab to browse through topics by category.

Click the Index tab to see a list of index entries: either type the word you're looking for or scroll through the list.

Click the Find tab to search for words or phrases that may be contained in a Help topic.

2 If your Help file doesn't have a Contents tab, click the Contents button to see a list of topics.

Tip

• For more information about the items on each tab, click ? at the top of the dialog box, and then click the item.

Take the Windows Tour

1 Click the Contents tab.

2 Double-click the Tour topic.

3 Follow the directions to learn more Windows basics.

Use "What's This?" Help

1 In any Windows dialog box, click the "What's This?" Help button.

2 Click the item you want more information about.

3 Read the Help information, and then click anywhere to close Help.

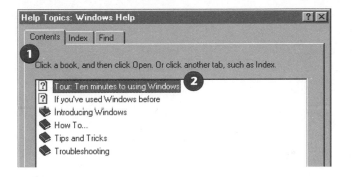

Quitting Windows

Shutting down your computer used to be a simple matter—you just turned it *off!* But in Windows 95, just as starting the computer takes longer, shutting it down takes more time while Windows closes any open programs and saves all your current settings.

TIP

Some computers with advanced power-management features shut off automatically after you confirm that you want to shut down the computer.

TIP

You'll want to restart Windows if you have software problems or when you've made changes to the configuration.

SEE ALSO

"Quitting When You're Stuck" on page 75 if you have problems when you try to quit Windows.

Shut Down and Turn Off Your Computer

1 Click the Start button, and choose Shut Down.

2 Click the appropriate option.

3 Click Yes.

Reloads Windows.

Exits Windows. Wait for a message telling you that it's safe to turn off your computer.

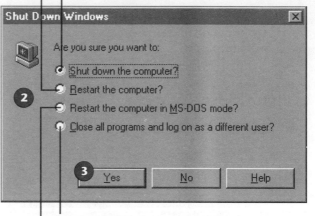

Shut Down Windows

Are you sure you want to:

Shut down the computer?

Restart the computer?

Restart the computer in MS-DOS mode?

Close all programs and log on as a different user?

Yes   No   Help

Resets Windows for a new user to log on.

Exits Windows and restarts the computer in MS-DOS mode.

Dialog Box Decisions

You're going to be seeing a lot of *dialog boxes* as you use Windows, and if you're not familiar with them now, you soon will be. Dialog boxes appear when Windows or a program (WordPad, let's say) needs you to make one or more decisions about what you want to do. Sometimes all you have to do is click a Yes or No button; at other times, there'll be quite a few decisions to make in one dialog box. The Print dialog box, shown below, is one you'll probably be seeing frequently, so take a look at its components and how they work.

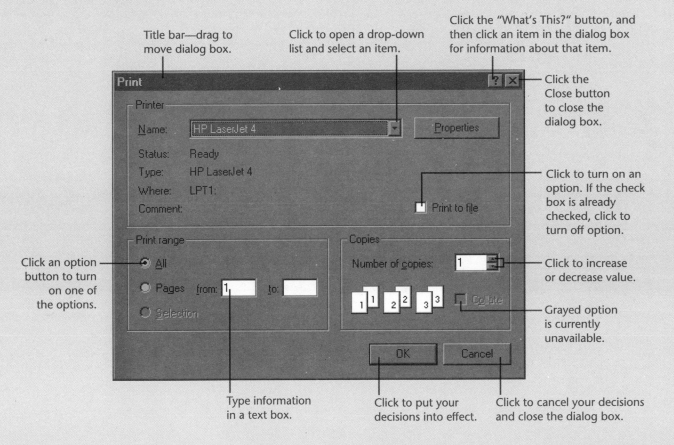

2

Title bar—drag to move dialog box.

Click to open a drop-down list and select an item.

Click the "What's This?" button, and then click an item in the dialog box for information about that item.

Click the Close button to close the dialog box.

Click to turn on an option. If the check box is already checked, click to turn off option.

Click an option button to turn on one of the options.

Click to increase or decrease value.

Grayed option is currently unavailable.

Type information in a text box.

Click to put your decisions into effect.

Click to cancel your decisions and close the dialog box.

3

Navigating Windows

Using Windows 95 is like having a super-efficient office assistant. When you open a folder on the Windows Desktop, Windows shows you an inventory of every document, or file, in the folder. When you tell Windows what you want to do, it hurries off to do your bidding—fetch a file, copy a document and put the copy away in another folder, toss old files into the Recycle Bin, and so on. And, of course, Windows always updates the inventory of your folder whenever the contents change.

The filing system in Windows is structured like a paper-filing system, with one huge difference: *Windows remembers where everything belongs*. With a paper-filing system, *you* have to do the remembering! *You* have to remember to put your Mortgage Payments Records back in the Budget folder that's inside the Household folder that's located in the second drawer of the filing cabinet. With Windows, all you have to do is grab your Mortgage Payments Records document from the Budget folder, and when you've finished with it, *Windows* puts it back in the Budget folder that's inside the Household folder that's located on your hard drive.

Of course, Windows can't read your mind—you have to give it some information to work with, so in this section we'll explore the tools and shortcuts that Windows provides to help you get your work done.

Exploring Windows

Sitting on the Windows Desktop is the gateway (okay, it's a window) to your computer. It's called, appropriately enough, My Computer. Using My Computer, you open windows to the world of *your* computer, and you can move to any folder and find any file anywhere on your computer.

TIP

To move back to the previous window, press Backspace.

SEE ALSO

"Mouse Maneuvers" on page 14 for information about pointing, clicking, double-clicking, and dragging with the mouse.

Open a Folder

1. Double-click My Computer on the Windows Desktop.

2. Double-click a drive icon (for example, [C:]) to open a window for that drive.

3. Double-click a folder icon (for example, My Documents) to open a window for that folder.

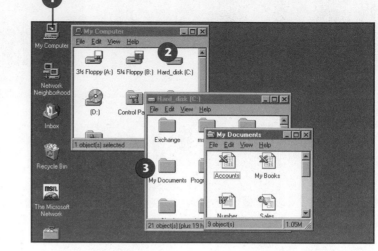

Move an Icon

1. Point to the file icon.

2. Drag the file icon and drop it at a new location.

3. Whether you're using Small Icons view or Large Icons view, choose Line Up Icons from the window's View menu to keep those icons in line!

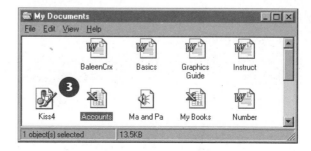

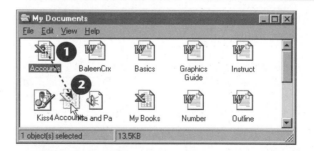

SEE ALSO

"Managing Files with Windows Explorer" on page 56 for information about managing folders and files with Windows Explorer.

TRY THIS

Window Treatments. *Point to Arrange Icons on the window's View menu, and then choose Auto Arrange from the submenu (if there's not already a check mark next to it) to turn on Auto Arrange mode. Auto Arrange mode moves the icons to fill any gaps left when an icon is moved or deleted, adds space if the icons become too crowded, and rearranges the icons to fit a window that has been resized.*

TIP

If you want to close a series of windows in one fell swoop, hold down the Shift key while you click the Close button on the last window opened—all the windows that are on the direct route back from that last window to My Computer will close.

Change the Display

1 Click the View menu.

2 Choose a view.

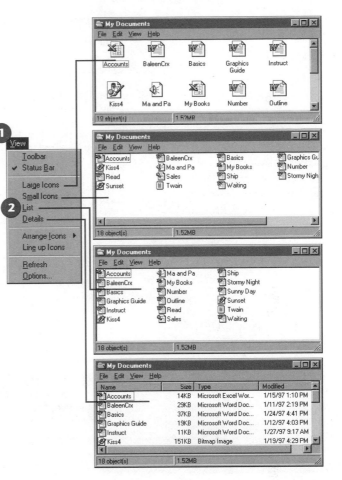

Sorting the File Listings

Depending on the contents of your files and your own idiosyncrasies, you might want Windows to list files alphabetically, by date of most recent edit, by size, or by some other criterion. Windows can also reverse the sorting order—listing names from Z to A, for example—in an opened window.

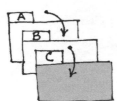

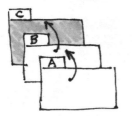

Sort the Files

1 Double-click My Computer on the Windows Desktop.

2 Open the folder you want to examine.

3 Click the View menu and point to Arrange Icons.

4 From the submenu, choose the type of sorting you want:

◆ By Name to order the files by their filenames

◆ By Type to order the files by their type—Word, Excel, Paint, and so on

◆ By Size to order the files by their size in kilobytes

◆ By Date to order the files by the date they were created or most recently modified

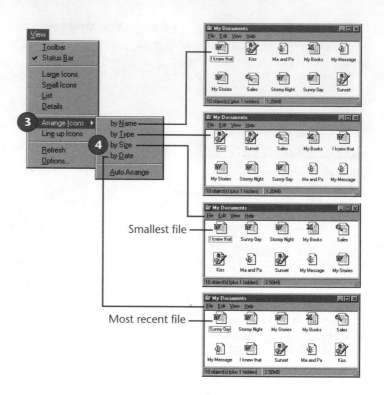

Smallest file

Most recent file

SEE ALSO

"Locating a File by Name" on page 30 and "Locating a File by Date or Content" on page 32 for information about finding files.

TRY THIS

If you don't have a folder open, double-click the My Computer icon, double-click the C: drive, double-click My Documents, and choose Details from the View menu. Click the Type button to see all the files grouped by their types. Then click the Name button to list the files alphabetically.

Reverse the Sort Order

1. Choose Details from the View menu.

2. Click a label button (Name, Size, Type, or Modified) to choose the type of sorting you want.

3. Click the same label button to reverse the sort order.

Smallest file   Click the Size button to sort by file size.

Name	Size	Type	Modified
I knew that	5KB	Microsoft Word Doc...	1/2/97 2:08 PM
Sunny Day	12KB	Microsoft Word Doc...	1/30/97 2:46 PM
Stormy Night	12KB	Microsoft Word Doc...	1/30/97 2:46 PM
My Books	26KB	Microsoft Excel Wor...	1/27/97 9:17 AM
Sales	72KB	Microsoft Access Da...	1/15/97 1:10 PM
Kiss	151KB	Bitmap Image	1/15/97 1:10 PM
Ma and Pa	206KB	Wave Sound	1/12/97 4:03 PM
Sunset	302KB	Bitmap Image	1/18/97 2:30 PM
My Message	435KB	Wave Sound	1/10/97 5:04 AM
My Stories	1,344KB	Microsoft Word Doc...	1/25/97 12:37 PM

10 object(s) (plus 1 hidden)   2.50MB

Largest file

Name	Size	Type	Modified
My Stories	1,344KB	Microsoft Word Doc...	1/25/97 12:37 PM
My Message	435KB	Wave Sound	1/10/97 5:04 AM
Sunset	302KB	Bitmap Image	1/18/97 2:30 PM
Ma and Pa	206KB	Wave Sound	1/12/97 4:03 PM
Kiss	151KB	Bitmap Image	1/15/97 1:10 PM
Sales	72KB	Microsoft Access Da...	1/15/97 1:10 PM
My Books	26KB	Microsoft Excel Wor...	1/27/97 9:17 AM
Stormy Night	12KB	Microsoft Word Doc...	1/30/97 2:46 PM
Sunny Day	12KB	Microsoft Word Doc...	1/30/97 2:46 PM
I knew that	5KB	Microsoft Word Doc...	1/2/97 2:08 PM

10 object(s) (plus 1 hidden)   2.50MB

Gaining Access to Everything

The My Computer window gives you easy access to the drives on your computer, but you can also use it to access the contents of your Windows Desktop, of other computers in your workgroup, and even of your network resources.

Display the Toolbar

1. Double-click My Computer on the Windows Desktop.

2. Choose Toolbar from the View menu to display the toolbar.

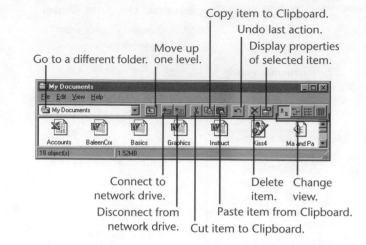

Go to a different folder.
Move up one level.
Copy item to Clipboard.
Undo last action.
Display properties of selected item.

Connect to network drive.
Disconnect from network drive.
Cut item to Clipboard.
Delete item.
Change view.
Paste item from Clipboard.

Choose a Different Location

1. Click the down arrow at the right of the Go To A Different Folder box to open the drop-down list.

2. Click the new location to display it in the current window.

Folders and the File Structure

As we mentioned at the beginning of this section, the filing system in Windows is structured very much like a paper-filing system: My Computer is the filing cabinet; the drives are the drawers of the filing cabinet; the folders in the drives are the folders in the drawers, and sometimes, in each system, there are folders inside folders. And, just as with the paper-filing system, you store your documents, or files, inside the folders.

Windows maintains the basic structure for you—My Computer, the drives, the folders for your programs, and even a single folder to hold all your documents—but if you want to organize your files with a little more detail, you can create your own series of folders to define your own structure.

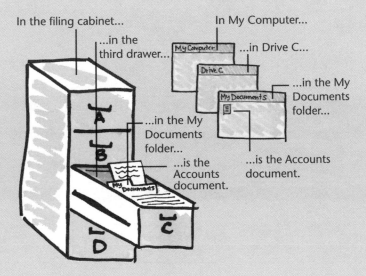

In the filing cabinet...

...in the third drawer...

...in the My Documents folder...

...is the Accounts document.

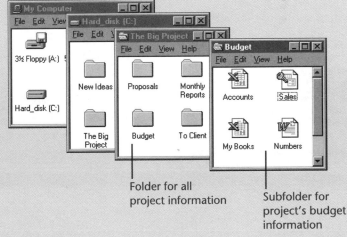

In My Computer...

...in Drive C...

...in the My Documents folder...

...is the Accounts document.

Folder for all project information

Subfolder for project's budget information

Arranging Windows on the Desktop

When you open a series of windows to get to a specific file or folder, your Desktop can become littered with overlapping windows. You can close each window that you don't need and arrange the open windows for easy access. If you want to be *really* neat, set My Computer to use only one window, which changes as it displays each folder.

TIP

Use a single window if you keep all your documents for a project in one folder and usually work in one folder at a time. Use a separate window for each folder if you use documents from different folders or if you frequently copy documents between folders.

Arrange Your Open Windows

1. Minimize any windows other than the ones you want displayed.

2. Point to an empty spot on the Windows taskbar and right-click.

3. Choose Cascade, Tile Horizontally, or Tile Vertically to arrange all the open windows.

Use a Single Window

1. Choose Options from the View menu.

2. Click the Folder tab.

3. Select the Browsing option that lets you use a single window that changes as you open each folder.

4. Click OK.

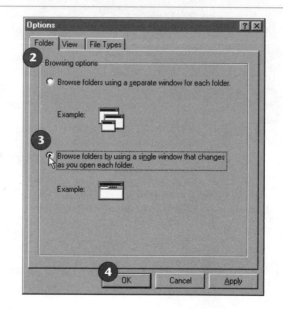

Getting More Information About a File or Folder

Windows records information and statistics on every file and folder that you can access from Windows. The information depends on the type of file or what's contained in the folder. This information is called the file's or the folder's *properties*.

TIP

Unless you have a good reason to do so, don't change the Attributes settings. Programs use this information in their own file-management processes, and changes can cause unexpected results.

SEE ALSO

"Locating a File by Name" on page 30 for information about locating files or folders.

"Starting an MS-DOS–Based Program from Windows" on page 108 for information about setting properties for MS-DOS files.

Review the Properties of a File or Folder

1. Find the file or folder you want to examine.

2. Right-click the file or folder.

3. Choose Properties from the submenu.

4. Review the information in the Properties dialog box.

5. Click OK.

Different types of documents have different tabs.

Change attributes if necessary.

Shows size taken up by all files, including those in subfolders.

Change attributes if necessary.

3

Locating a File by Name

If you don't know where a file is located, you can waste a lot of time trying to find it no matter which method you use to explore your windows. Fortunately, Windows can find it for you.

TIP

If you don't know the full name of the file or folder you're looking for, enter as much as you know, and Windows will find files that use the characters you typed.

TIP

Depending on the programs you have installed, you can use the Find command to search other locations. For example, you can use it to search the Microsoft Network if you are an MSN member, or you can use Outlook for advanced searches if you have Microsoft Office 97 installed.

Find a Folder or a File Somewhere on Your Computer

1 Click the Start button, point to Find, and choose Files Or Folders from the submenu.

2 Type the name, or as much of it as you can remember, in the Named box.

3 Select the location to be searched.

4 Turn on the Include Subfolders check box to search all subfolders.

5 Click Find Now.

6 Examine the results.

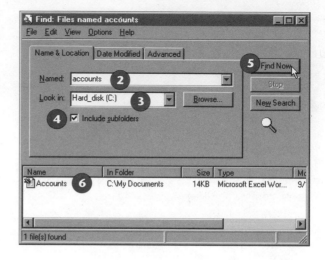

Limit the Search to a Specific Location

1 Click the Browse button.

2 Select the folder to search, and click OK.

3 Turn off the Include Subfolders check box unless you want to include the subfolders in the folder you specified.

4 Click Find Now.

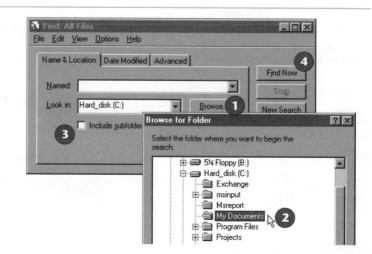

Shut Out! *You might be unable to locate some files on a network even though you know those files are there. Access privileges set on the workgroup host computer or by the network administrator might make these files inaccessible to you.*

"Editing Text Documents in WordPad" on page 64 for information about cutting and copying text.

"Viewing a Document Quickly" on page 73 for information about Quick View.

"Placing Shortcuts on the Desktop" on page 122 for information about creating shortcuts.

Find a File on a Network

1. Click the Browse button.

2. Select a server, a workgroup computer, or a folder on the server or workgroup computer, and click OK.

3. Click Find Now.

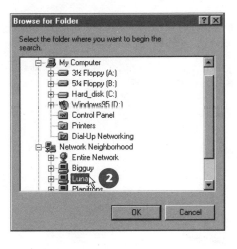

Use the Found File

1. Point to the file and right-click.

2. Choose the appropriate command.

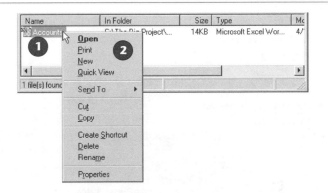

Locating a File by Date or Content

You can search for a file by the date when it was last saved, by text contained in the file, or by file type. You can use any of these as your sole search criterion, or use them in conjunction with the file's name and location.

SEE ALSO

"Locating a File by Name" on page 30 for information about specifying the name and location, and "Conducting and Reusing a Search" on the opposite page for information about saving searches and search results.

TIP

A Sensitive Case. *If you want to search for content that exactly matches the uppercase and lowercase letters you typed in the Containing Text field, choose the Case Sensitive command from the Options menu.*

Find a File by Its Date

1. Click the Start button, point to Find, and choose Files Or Folders from the submenu.

2. Click the Date Modified tab.

3. Select the range of dates to search.

4. Click Find Now.

Search restricted to specified date range   First day of range   Last day of range

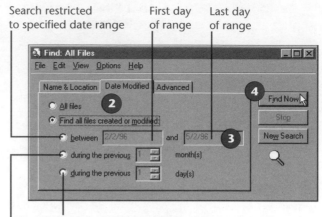

Search restricted to range from current date to specified number of days ago

Search restricted to range from current date to specified number of months ago

Find a File by Its Type, Content, or Size

1. Click the Advanced tab.

2. Enter the search information.

3. Click Find Now.

Select type of file or folder.

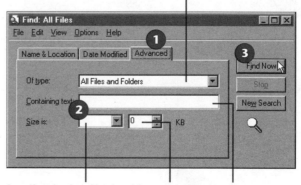

Specify whether file should be larger or smaller than specified value.

Specify size threshold.

Enter text contained in the file.

Conducting and Reusing a Search

If you conduct a search and want to use the search results at a later time, or if you frequently conduct a search using the same criteria, you can save the search and its results for later use.

Set Up and Conduct a Search

1 Click the Start button, point to Find, and choose Files Or Folders.

2 Enter your search criteria in the Find dialog box and click Find Now.

Save the Search and Its Results

1 Choose Save Results from the Options menu if there's not already a check mark next to it.

2 Choose Save Search from the File menu.

Check mark shows that search results will be saved with search.

Reuse a Search

1 Double-click the search results on the Windows Desktop.

2 Use the results of the previous search or rerun the search to update the list.

Organizing Your Folders

Windows provides the basic filing structure for you—drives and ready-made folders such as My Documents and Printers. You can customize the filing system by adding your own folders, or even adding folders inside folders (subfolders).

TIP

Off Limits! *There are some locations in which you can't create your own folders—for example, the My Computer window, the Printers and Control Panel folders, or any network folder to which you don't have full access. In these cases, the New command won't be on the submenu.*

Create a Folder

1. Open the window of the destination folder, drive, or other location.

2. Point to an empty part of the window and right-click.

3. Point to New.

4. Choose Folder.

5. Type a name, and press Enter.

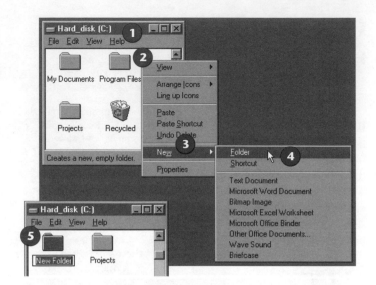

Move or Copy a Folder into Another Folder

1. Open the window containing the folder to be moved or copied.

2. Open the destination folder.

3. Select the folder to be moved or copied.

4. To move the folder, drag it and drop it in the destination-folder window. To copy the folder, hold down the Ctrl key while dragging.

Plus sign shows the folder is being copied.

Renaming or Deleting a Folder

It's quick and easy to rename your folders if you need to, or to edit a folder name that you might have misspelled. Deleting a folder is even easier—in fact, it's *so* easy that Windows asks you for confirmation. However, if you delete a folder and then suddenly realize that you shouldn't have deleted it, don't panic—you can usually retrieve it from the Recycle Bin.

SEE ALSO

"Recovering a Deleted Item" on page 42 for information about retrieving a deleted folder from the Recycle Bin.

Rename a Folder

1. Click the folder to select it.

2. Click the folder name (not the folder icon).

3. With the name selected, type a new name, or click to position the insertion point and then edit the name.

4. Press Enter.

Delete a Folder

1. Open the drive or folder containing the folder to be deleted.

2. Select the folder.

3. Press the Delete key.

4. Click Yes to delete the folder or file and send it to the Recycle Bin.

5. If you are deleting a folder that contains files, click the appropriate button if Windows asks you to confirm the deletion of some types of files.

Terminates deletion. Folder and remaining files aren't deleted.

Deletes file.

Deletes all files of this type.

Skips deletion of this file and folder.

Organizing Your Files

If you have a limited number of files, you can easily keep them all in the My Documents folder that Windows provides. However, if you have many files or files dealing with different projects, you'll probably want to organize them by placing them in individual folders.

TIP

Use the Shift to Shift!
When you drag a file to a folder that's on a different drive, Windows copies the file but doesn't move it. To move it, hold down the Shift key while you drag the file.

Move a File into a Subfolder

1 Open the window containing the file and the subfolder.

2 Select the file to be moved.

3 Drag the file and drop it on top of the subfolder.

Move a File into Another Folder

1 Open the window containing the file to be moved.

2 Open the destination folder.

3 Select the file to be moved.

4 Drag the file to the destination folder and drop it on a blank spot.

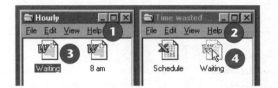

TIP

To select a series of contiguous files, click the first file, hold down the Shift key, and then click the last file.

SEE ALSO

"Exploring Windows with Windows Explorer" on page 54 for information about moving files among several different folders.

Copy a File into a Folder

1 Open the window containing the file to be copied.

2 Open the destination folder.

3 Select the file to be copied.

4 Hold down the Ctrl key, drag the file to the destination folder, and drop the file's copy on a blank spot.

Move or Copy Several Files

1 Select the files to be moved or copied.

2 Point to any one of the selected files, holding down the Ctrl key if the files are to be copied, and then drag the files and drop them at the new location.

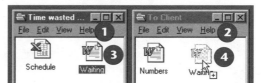

1 Select the files you want to move or copy. Hold down the Ctrl key and click to select multiple files.

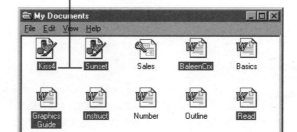

Storing Information on a Floppy Disk

If you use floppy disks to transport or archive information, Windows provides easy access to your disks. If you have a disk that's not preformatted, or if you want to quickly erase and reuse a disk, you'll need to format the disk before you can use it.

TIP

Look Before You Delete!
When you're duplicating a disk, any existing information on the destination disk will be deleted, so check the contents of the disk before using it.

TIP

Always label both disks before you duplicate a disk, to make sure that you don't use the same disk as both source and destination disk.

Format a Floppy Disk

1. Place the disk in your floppy drive.

2. Double-click My Computer on the Windows Desktop.

3. Right-click the floppy drive.

4. Choose Format from the shortcut menu.

5. Choose the formatting option(s) you want:

   ◆ Quick (Erase) to erase the directory and overwrite all files on the disk

   ◆ Full for disks that have not been formatted before, or are formatted differently

   ◆ Copy System Files Only to add the operating system files to the disk

6. Type a name for the disk if you want one (up to 11 characters long), and make any changes you want under Other Options.

7. Click Start.

8. Click Close when formatting has been completed.

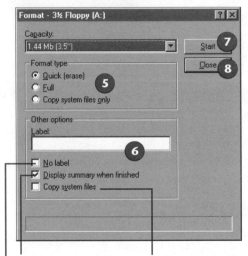

Shows a summary to verify the formatting.

Adds system files to the disk you're formatting.

Removes label from disk.

To see how much free space you have on a floppy disk, place the disk in the drive, open your My Computer window, right-click the floppy drive, and choose Properties from the shortcut menu. The General tab displays the amounts of used and free space.

Copy Files or Folders to a Floppy Disk

1 Place a disk in your floppy drive.

2 Open the window containing the files or folders to be copied.

3 Select the files or folders to be copied.

4 Right-click a selected file or folder.

5 Point to Send To on the shortcut menu.

6 Click the floppy drive that contains the disk.

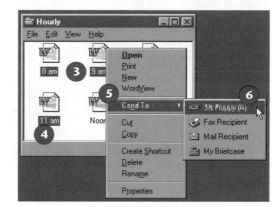

Duplicate a Floppy Disk

1 Place the disk to be duplicated in your floppy drive.

2 Open the My Computer window, right-click the drive containing the disk, and point to Copy Disk on the shortcut menu.

3 Select the drives to be used.

4 Click Start.

5 Click Close when copying has been completed.

You can copy only between drives of the same type. If you're using a single drive, switch disks when requested.

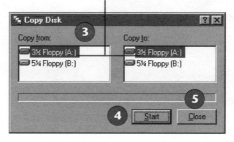

Creating and Working with Shortcuts

If you use a particular folder or file frequently, you can access it quickly by putting a shortcut to it on the Windows Desktop or on the Start menu. A shortcut to a document opens the file; a shortcut to a program file starts that program; a shortcut to a folder opens the folder in a window.

TIP

You can also create shortcuts to network locations.

SEE ALSO

"Creating Quick Access to a Network Resource" on page 171 for information about creating shortcuts to network locations.

Create a Shortcut to a Folder or File

1. Open the window containing the folder or file.

2. Right-click the folder or file.

3. Choose Create Shortcut from the shortcut menu.

4. Drag the shortcut and drop it on the Windows Desktop.

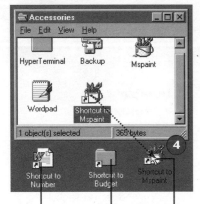

Opens the file in Word.   Opens the folder in a window.   Starts the Paint program.

SEE ALSO

"Adding an Item to the Start Menu" on page 153 for more information about adding items to the Start menu.

TRY THIS

Create a folder and fill it with shortcuts to your favorite locations. Then create a shortcut to this folder and place it on your Desktop. Without cluttering up your Desktop, you now have access to many shortcuts.

Move a Shortcut to the Start Menu

1 Drag the shortcut and drop it on top of the Start button.

2 Click the Start button to verify that the shortcut is on the Start menu.

Delete a Shortcut from the Windows Desktop

1 Click the shortcut on the Windows Desktop.

2 Press the Delete key.

3 Click Yes to delete the shortcut and send it to the Recycle Bin.

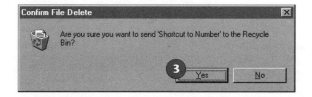

Recovering a Deleted Item

If you delete a file, folder, or shortcut by mistake, you can quickly recover it by either undoing your action or restoring the deleted item from the Recycle Bin. The Recycle Bin holds all the files you've deleted from your hard drive(s) until you empty the bin or until it gets so full that the oldest files are automatically deleted.

SEE ALSO

"Saving Disk Space by Frequent Recycling" on page 145 for more information about changing the size of your Recycle Bin.

TIP

When you delete an entire folder and its contents, all the files contained in the folder are shown in the Recycle Bin, but the folder isn't shown. If you restore any of the files, Windows cleverly re-creates the folder and places the restored files in the folder.

Undo a Deletion

1. Point to an empty part of the Windows Desktop or to an empty part of any folder window, and right-click.

2. Choose Undo Delete from the shortcut menu.

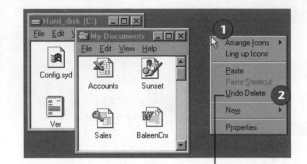

Available only if the deletion was your last action

Restore an Item from the Recycle Bin

1. Double-click the Recycle Bin icon on the Windows Desktop.

2. Select the item or items to be recovered, and right-click.

3. Choose Restore from the shortcut menu.

4. Click the Close button to close the Recycle Bin.

Displaying MS-DOS Information

You can display standard MS-DOS information—paths and filename extensions—as you navigate through folders.

SEE ALSO

Section 7, "Running MS-DOS," starting on page 101, for information about working in MS-DOS.

Display MS-DOS Information

1. Double-click My Computer on the Windows Desktop.

2. Choose Options from the View menu.

3. Click the View tab.

4. Turn on the Display The Full MS-DOS Path In The Title Bar check box.

5. Turn off the Hide MS-DOS File Extensions For File Types That Are Registered check box.

6. Click OK.

MS-DOS path in title bar

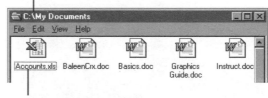

Filename includes MS-DOS filename extension.

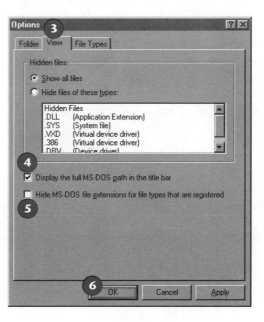

3

Hiding System Files

"Why would I want to hide files?" you ask. There's a good reason for the cloak-and-dagger stuff. The files you'll hide are used by the operating system and by some of your programs, and you'll rarely—*if ever*—want to move, delete, or rename any of them. By hiding them, you protect yourself from the horrors that can occur when a critical file is accidentally deleted. Tuck the files away out of sight and forget about them. The files still exist in their folders, the programs that need to access them can still find them, and you and your computer will live happily ever after.

Hide System Files

1. Choose Options from the View menu.

2. Click the View tab.

3. Click the Hide Files Of These Types option button.

4. Click OK.

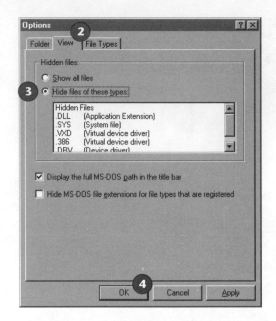

System files displayed

System files hidden

4

Working with Programs

Getting to know the programs that come with Windows 95 is a bit like moving into a new house or apartment. Just as your new abode has the basics—stove, refrigerator, bathtub, and (dare we say it?) windows—the Windows operating system comes with several useful accessories and tools. Just as you'll add dishes, furniture, rugs, and all the other accoutrements that turn empty rooms into a home, you'll add other programs to Windows to utilize its full potential as you work (and play).

But take a look at the basics first. There's WordPad, a handy little word processor for quick notes, and Paint, an easy-to-use graphics program. You'll meet Windows Explorer—the alternative to using My Computer to manage your files. Windows comes with other goodies, too: mail and fax capabilities, multimedia, and lots of accessory programs—but we'll save those for later. Right now we'll cover some quick ways to accomplish everyday tasks: switching between multiple programs with a single mouse-click, for example, and copying items between documents that were created in different programs.

And, just as you might customize the walls of your living quarters with paintings or wallpaper, you can have some fun redecorating your Windows Desktop with your own highly individual "wallpaper" creations.

Managing Multiple Programs

Windows lets you run several programs at the same time. You can have more than one open program window on your screen and can easily switch between programs. If you prefer, you can park your running programs neatly on the taskbar, where they'll sit snoozing quietly until you need them. To make one or all of them instantly spring back to life on your screen, just click their program buttons.

Switch Between Program Windows

1 If you have several overlapping program windows on your screen, click in any visible part of an open window to bring it to the front of your screen and make it the active program—that is, the program you're working on now.

2 If the program window is minimized or is obscured by other windows, click the program button on the taskbar.

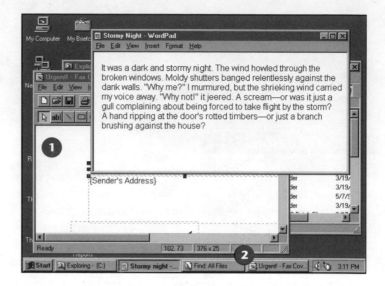

Windows, and
Windows in Windows

Windows is called "Windows" because everything in Windows is contained in a window. Well, almost everything. In Windows 95, the icons on the Desktop have escaped from their windows, and the taskbar and the Start menu are free of window restraints. There are a few other items that work outside of windows, too— some toolbars and dialog boxes, and the Setup wizards that Windows uses to install new hardware and change system settings. But, by and large, every program lives in a window. Some programs even have windows inside their window.

WordPad and Microsoft Word are good examples of the difference between a program that uses a single window and one that uses *document windows*.

Document windows work just like program windows, except that when you close a document window, you are closing only the document or the file that lives in that window; the main program window stays open. Likewise, when you move, size, maximize, or minimize a document window, it is still contained within the program window.

Most programs that have document windows also have a Window menu that you can use to arrange the windows and to switch between them.

WordPad can display only
one document at a time.

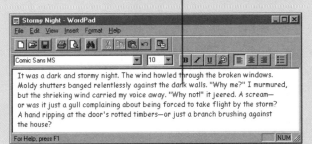

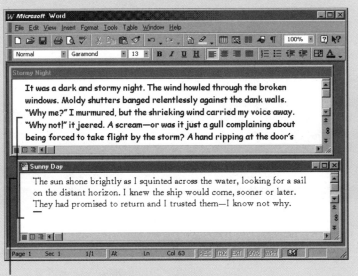

Word can display different documents in
separate windows within the Word window.

Copying Material Between Documents

It's easy to copy material from a document that was created in one program to a document that was created in another program. How you insert the material depends on what it is. If it's similar to and compatible with the receiving document—text that's being copied into a Word document, for example—it's usually inserted as is and can be edited in the receiving document's program. If the item is dissimilar—a sound clip, say, inserted into a Word document—it's either *encapsulated*, or isolated, as an object and can be edited in the originating program only, or you simply are not able to paste that item into your document.

Copy and Insert Material

1 In the source document, select the material to be copied.

2 Choose Copy from the Edit menu. Windows places copied items on the Clipboard. You can copy only one item at a time, so always paste the Clipboard contents into your document before you copy anything else, or you'll lose whatever was on the Clipboard.

3 Switch to the destination document.

4 Click where you want to insert the material.

5 Choose Paste from the Edit menu.

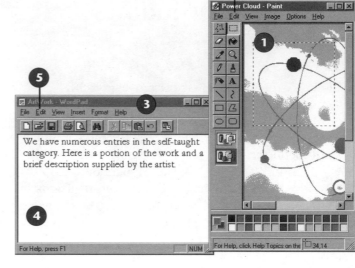

Copy and Insert an Entire Document

1 Use My Computer to locate and select the document to be copied.

2 Drag the document to the destination document, and drop it where you want it to appear.

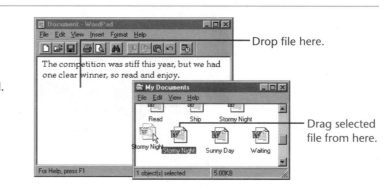

Drop file here.

Drag selected file from here.

Editing Inserted Material

When material from a document that was created in a different program has been inserted in your document as an *embedded object*, you can edit the inserted item *in place*—that is, in your document—using the tools of the program it which it was created.

TIP

Some programs won't let you edit inserted material in place. Instead, the source program opens automatically and you can make your edits there. When you've finished, choose the Update command from the source program's File menu to update the information in the embedded object before you exit the source program.

Edit Inserted Material in Place

1 Double-click the inserted item.

2 Use the toolbar buttons, menu commands, and whatever other tools are provided by the source program to make your editing changes.

3 Click outside the selected area to return the material back into the embedded object and to restore the toolbars, menus, and other tools of your original program.

Paint menus
Paint tools
WordPad window
Paint program activated in WordPad window

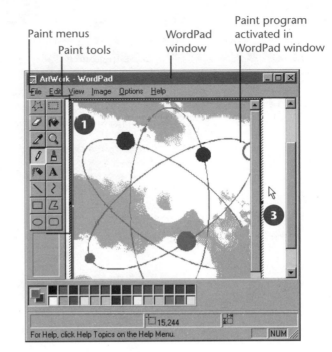

4

Linking to Information That Changes

When the content of an item you've inserted into your document is likely to change in the source document, you can make sure that those changes are automatically updated in your document. You do this by *linking* to the source document. When the content of the source document changes, the changes appear in your document. But because the content resides in the source document and not in your document, the source document must be available whenever you work in your document. If you change the location of the source document, you must change the link, because the link contains the full path to the document.

Link to a Source Document

1 Locate the source document and right-click it.

2 Choose Copy from the shortcut menu.

3 Switch to the destination document.

4 Click at the location where you want to insert the item.

5 Choose Paste Special from the Edit menu.

6 Select the Paste Link option.

7 Click OK.

Source document

Check to display icon instead of content.

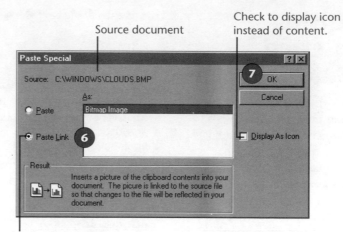

Links the inserted content to an external document.

*What happens if the source
document is no longer available depends on your program.
If the linked item remains in
your document but its content
is never updated, your program
converted the item into an
embedded object; you'll need to
relink the item to the source
document. If you get a message
telling you that the file can't be
found, or if a different document appears, use the Change
Source button in the Links
dialog box to locate the source
document and reestablish the
link to the correct document
at the correct location.*

Change the Link

1 In your document, select the linked information.

2 Choose Links from the Edit menu.

3 Select the current link.

4 Make the changes.

Click to browse and locate moved document, or to use different document.

Click to edit document in its source program.

Current link

Links

Links:
C:\WINDOWS\Circles.bmp   Type: Bitmap Image   Update: Automatic

Cancel

Update Now — Click to update content from source document.

Open Source

Change Source...

Break Link

Source: C:\WINDOWS\Circles.bmp
Type: Bitmap Image
Update: ● Automatic   ○ Manual

Automatically updates link.

Updates link only at your command.

Click to disconnect from source document. Content becomes embedded in your document.

4

Creating a Document

You can create and name a blank document for any of the programs you have installed. When you're ready to get to work, you simply double-click the document, and it opens, ready for you to add content. This way, the document is named and located in the correct folder—and you don't need to look around for the program and open it.

Create a Document

1. Open the folder that is to contain the new document.

2. Point to an empty part of the window and right-click.

3. Choose New from the shortcut menu.

4. Click a document type.

5. Type a name for the new document, and press Enter.

Windows lists documents only for programs that are installed.

Double-click to open the document.

Meet Windows Explorer

Windows Explorer has functions similar to those of the folder windows that you reach from My Computer. The list of computers, disks, and folders (often called a *directory tree*) in the left pane gives you direct access to any drive or folder on your computer or on a network. You can click the plus sign next to a drive or folder name to *expand* that branch of the tree structure and see the subfolders, and then click the minus sign to *collapse* the branch and hide the subfolders again. The right pane shows you the contents of whatever item you select in the left pane.

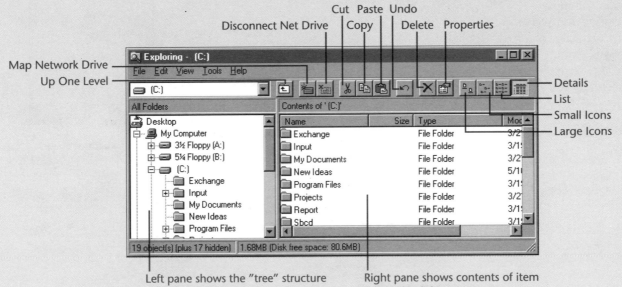

Map Network Drive
Up One Level

Disconnect Net Drive

Cut Paste Undo
Copy   Delete Properties

Details
List
Small Icons
Large Icons

Left pane shows the "tree" structure in outline form.

Right pane shows contents of item selected in left pane.

4

Exploring Windows with Windows Explorer

If you're new to Windows, take a few minutes to go exploring with Windows Explorer. If you're a long-time Windows user, and you liked using File Manager in Windows version 3, you'll feel right at home with Windows Explorer.

SEE ALSO

"Managing Files with Windows Explorer" on page 56 for information about copying and moving files and folders with Windows Explorer.

Explore

1. Click the Start button, point to Programs, and choose Windows Explorer from the submenu.

2. Click through the drives and folders in the left pane to reach the folder that you want to explore. Use the plus or minus signs to display or hide subfolders.

3. Click any folder to see a listing of its contents displayed in the right pane.

Click a plus sign to expand the listing and display the folders it contains.

Click a minus sign to collapse the listing and hide the folders it contains.

Click a folder... ...to see what it contains.

Searching for a File with Windows Explorer

If you want to find a file but don't know its exact location, you can search for it in Windows Explorer. By starting in a specific folder you can narrow down the search and save yourself some time.

TIP

If you want to see the complete contents of a folder and the contents of all its subfolders, in one list, leave the Named field blank.

SEE ALSO

"Locating a File by Date or Content" on page 32 for information about completing the different tabs.

Search for a File

1 In the left pane, open the drive or folder that you know contains the file.

2 Choose Find from the Tools menu, and then choose Files Or Folders from the submenu.

3 Type the name of the file, or as much of it as you can remember.

4 Fill in as much information as you can on the Date Modified and Advanced tabs.

5 Click Find Now.

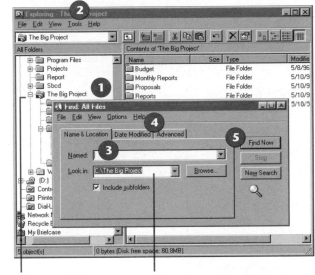

The open folder... ...determines where the search is started.

4

Managing Files with Windows Explorer

With Windows Explorer you can quickly and easily copy or move any files or folders on any drive that is accessible to your computer.

Copy or Move Files and Folders

1 Expand the drive and any folders to display the folder containing the files or folders to be moved or copied.

2 Click the folder to display its contents in the right pane.

3 Select the files or folders.

4 Drag and drop the files or folders into the destination folder:

- ◆ Hold down the Ctrl key while dragging to copy a file or folder to a folder on the same drive.

- ◆ Hold down the Shift key while dragging to move a file or folder to another drive.

Drop when destination folder becomes selected.

Multiple selected files to be copied

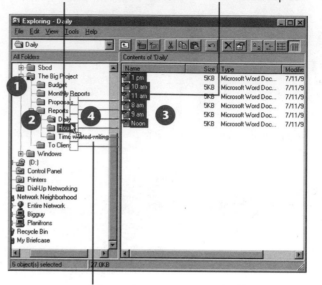

Files are being copied.

Create a Folder

1 Select the drive or folder that is to contain the new folder.

2 Right-click any blank spot in the right pane.

3 Choose New from the shortcut menu.

4 Choose Folder.

5 Type a name for the new folder, and press Enter.

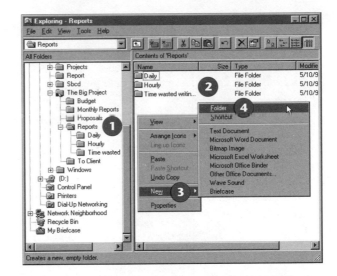

Deleting Files or Folders in Windows Explorer

You can quickly and easily delete any file or folder on any drive that is accessible to your computer. If you're deleting a file or folder from your hard disk, that file or folder is sent to the Recycle Bin. If you're deleting a file or folder from a floppy disk or from a network location, that file or folder is permanently deleted.

Delete a File or Folder

1. Select the file or folder on your computer to be deleted.

2. Press the Delete key.

3. Click Yes to delete the item and send it to the Recycle Bin.

4. If you're deleting a folder that contains files, click the appropriate button when Windows asks you to confirm the deletion of some types of files.

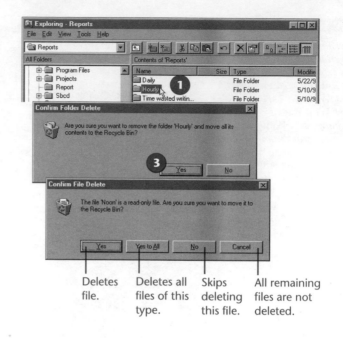

Deletes file.

Deletes all files of this type.

Skips deleting this file.

All remaining files are not deleted.

Customizing Windows Explorer

Just as you can customize the folder windows that you access from My Computer, you can change the look of Windows Explorer. By displaying only the window components that you use and changing the view, you can maximize your access to information.

SEE ALSO

"Displaying MS-DOS Information" on page 43 for information about displaying MS-DOS paths and filename extensions, and "Hiding System Files" on page 44 for information about hiding system files to avoid accidentally deleting them.

TIP

The type of view you choose affects only the right pane. You can't modify the view in the left pane.

Display or Hide Components

1 Click the View menu.

2 Choose a command to change the appearance of the window:

◆ Turn the Toolbar or Status Bar command on or off to display or hide the toolbar or status bar.

◆ Click a view to change the type of view.

3 Choose Options from the View menu, and on the View tab, turn the Include Description Bar For Right And Left Panes option on or off to display or hide the description bar.

Bullet indicates that List view is displayed.

Check mark indicates that status bar is displayed.

Description bar

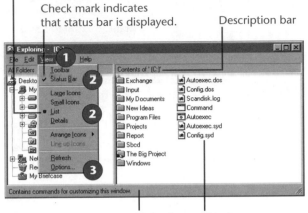

Status bar   List view

Resize the Panes

1 Position the mouse pointer over the border that separates the left and right panes, until the mouse pointer changes into the Resize pointer.

2 Drag the border to the left or right and drop it at a new location.

Drag the border to a new location.

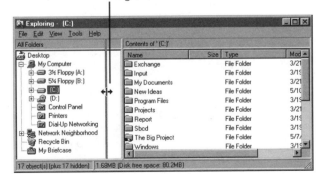

4

Creating a WordPad Document with Formatted Text

WordPad—a program that comes with Windows—can create and open Microsoft Word 6 documents, Rich Text Format (RTF) documents, and text documents. It can open but not create Windows Write documents. WordPad isn't a full-featured word processor, but it's ideal for quick notes. For anything more ambitious, you'll want to use a program such as Word.

Start WordPad, and Format the Page

1. Click the Start button, point to Programs and then to Accessories, and choose WordPad.

2. Choose Page Setup from the File menu to display the Page Setup dialog box.

3. Specify paper size, paper source, orientation, and margins.

4. Click OK.

5. Save the document.

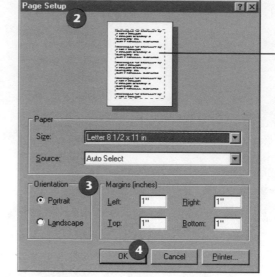

Portrait orientation, shown here, is a page that's longer than it is wide. Landscape orientation is a page that's wider than it is long.

Enter and Format Text

1. Use the View menu to display the Standard and the Formatting toolbars if they're not already visible.

2. Use the drop-down lists and buttons to format the text you're going to type.

3. Type your text.

4. Select any text you want to reformat, and use the formatting tools.

5. Save the document.

Click a "pushed-in" button to turn off formatting.

Click a button to turn on formatting.

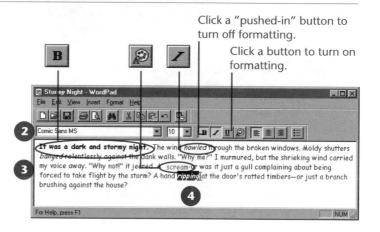

SEE ALSO

"Adding or Removing Windows Components" on page 156 for information about installing Windows components.

TIP

How Do You Measure Up?

You can use units other than inches. To set a different unit of measurement as the default, choose Options from the View menu and, on the Options tab, select the unit of measure you want.

TIP

Point to a button on any toolbar, and wait for a tooltip to appear to identify the button.

Format the Paragraphs

1 Choose Ruler from the View menu if the ruler isn't displayed.

2 Click in the paragraph to be formatted, or select all the paragraphs that you want to have the same formatting.

3 Use any of the formatting tools:

- ◆ Alignment buttons
- ◆ Bullets button
- ◆ Indent markers
- ◆ Tab markers

4 Save the document.

Drag for left indent.
Drag for first-line indent.
Click to set tab.
Click to set alignment.
Drag for right indent.

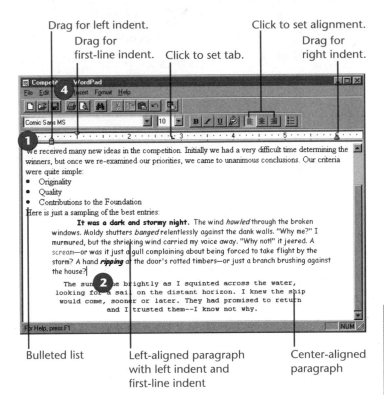

Bulleted list

Left-aligned paragraph with left indent and first-line indent

Center-aligned paragraph

Adding a Picture to a WordPad Document

You can create a picture in a program such as Paint and add it to a WordPad document, or you can add an existing picture from a picture file to a WordPad document. Either way, the picture is placed in WordPad as an object.

TIP

You can insert different types of objects, depending on the programs that are installed on your computer. The Object Type list shows the various types of objects supported by your system.

Create and Insert a Picture

1 Start WordPad, add and format your text, and position the insertion point where you want to place the picture.

2 Choose Object from the Insert menu to display the Insert Object dialog box.

3 Select the Create New option.

4 Select Bitmap Image as the Object Type.

5 Click OK.

6 Create a picture in the frame, using Paint's menus and controls, which temporarily replace WordPad's menus and controls.

7 Click outside the frame to deselect the object and return to WordPad.

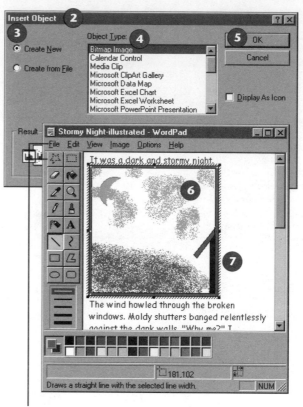

Paint's tools and menus are displayed in the WordPad window.

SEE ALSO

"Linking to Information That Changes" on page 50 for information about automatically updating information between documents.

"Creating a WordPad Document with Formatted Text" on page 60 for information about basic text formatting.

"Creating a Picture" on page 68 for detailed information about creating a picture in Paint.

TIP

After you've inserted a picture, you can verify that the document layout is correct by choosing Print Preview from the File menu.

Insert an Existing Picture

1. Click in the document where you want to place the picture.

2. Choose Object from the Insert menu.

3. Select Create From File.

4. Click Browse, find the picture file, and click Insert.

5. Click OK, and then click outside the frame to deselect the object and return to the document.

Turn on to link the file, or leave blank to embed the file. Document to insert

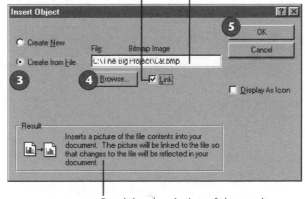

Read the description of the result.

Resize a Picture

1. Click the picture to select it.

2. Drag and drop a sizing handle to change the size of the picture.

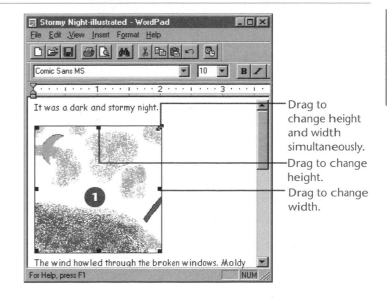

Drag to change height and width simultaneously.

Drag to change height.

Drag to change width.

4

Editing Text Documents in WordPad

You can use WordPad to edit Microsoft Word, Rich Text Format (RTF), or text-only (ANSI and ASCII) documents.

Open a Document

1. Start WordPad if it's not already running.

2. Click the Open button on the Toolbar.

3. Select the type of document to be opened.

4. Find and select the document.

5. Click Open.

Open dialog box

Look in: My Documents

Netlog
Stormy Night (4)
Twain
Ver

File name: Stormy Night   Open (5)

Files of type: Text Documents (3)   Cancel

Insert or Delete Text

1. Click where you want to insert the text.

2. Type the text.

3. Select text to be deleted by dragging the mouse pointer over the text.

4. Press the Delete key to delete the text.

1

It was a dark night. The wind nearly howled through the broken windows. Moldy shutters banged relentlessly against the dank walls. "Why me?" I murmured, but the

2

It was a dark and stormy night. The wind nearly howled through the broken windows. Moldy shutters banged relentlessly against the dank walls. "Why me?" I murmured,

3

It was a dark and stormy night. The wind nearly howled through the broken windows. Moldy shutters banged relentlessly against the dank walls. "Why me?" I murmured,

4

It was a dark and stormy night. The wind howled through the broken windows. Moldy shutters banged relentlessly against the dank walls. "Why me?" I murmured, but the

TIP

Presto Change-o. *To replace repetitive words or phrases throughout the document, use the Replace command on the Edit menu.*

Replace Text

1. Select the text to be replaced by dragging the mouse pointer over the text.

2. Type the new text. The selected text is deleted.

Selected text is replaced...

It was a dark and stormy night. The wind howled through the broken windows. Moldy shutters banged relentlessly against the **wet** walls. "Why me?" I murmured, but the

...when you type new text.

It was a dark and stormy night. The wind howled through the broken windows. Moldy shutters banged relentlessly against the dank walls. "Why me?" I murmured, but the

Move Text

1. Select the text to be moved by dragging the mouse pointer over the text.

2. Point to the selected text.

3. Drag the text and drop it in a new location.

Drag the selected text to a new location.

It was a dark and stormy night. The wind howled through the broken windows. Moldy shutters banged relentlessly against the dank walls. "Why me?" I murmured, but the **wind** shrieking carried my voice away. "Why not!" it jeered. A scream—or was it just a gull complaining about

It was a dark and stormy night. The wind howled through the broken windows. Moldy shutters banged relentlessly against the dank walls. "Why me?" I murmured, but the shrieking **wind** carried my voice away. "Why not!" it jeered. A scream—or was it just a gull complaining about

SEE ALSO

"Print a Document Using a Specific Printer" on page 74 to print your document using a printer other than the default printer.

Save and Print a Document

1. Click the Save button to save the document in the same format and with the same name.

2. Click the Print button to print the document using the default printer.

4

Creating a Text-Only Document

Text-only documents are useful in many circumstances. They are often used in program files (the well-known and dreaded INI and BAT files, for example), and they are useful when you're transferring information between documents that were created in different programs, because almost all word processors, editors, and viewers can read text-only files. A text-only document is exactly that: just bare-bones text with no formatting information. If you want to indent the paragraphs or apply bold or italic formatting, you'll need to save the document as a Word document or as an RTF document.

Start WordPad for Text

1. Start WordPad.

2. Choose New from the File menu to display the New dialog box.

3. Select Text Document.

4. Click OK.

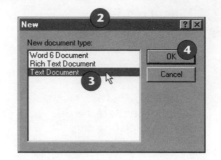

Customize Your View

1. Choose Options from the View menu to display the Options dialog box.

2. Click the Text tab.

3. Select the options for your display.

4. Click OK.

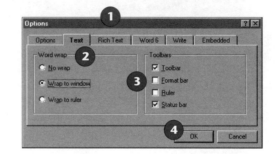

Create and Save Your Text

1. Type your text, pressing Enter when you want to start a new line.

2. Click the Save button

3. Open the folder where the document will be stored.

4. Type a filename. You can use up to 250 characters, including spaces, but you can't use the \ / * ? < > and | characters.

5. Save the document.

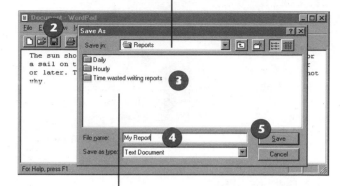

Shows folder that is open.

Keep double-clicking folders until you open the one you want.

Creating a Picture

If you're feeling artistic, you can create a picture in Paint. Paint comes with Windows and was designed to create and edit bitmap pictures. (A bitmap is just that: a map created from small dots, or *bits*. It's a lot like a piece of graph paper with some squares filled in and others left blank to create a picture.) Although you can print your picture if you want to, Paint pictures are usually inserted into other documents as embedded or linked objects. You can also create a Paint picture and use it as the wallpaper for your Windows Desktop.

SEE ALSO

"Copying Material Between Documents" on page 48 for information about embedding an object in a document.

"Linking to Information That Changes" on page 50 for information about linking an object.

Create a Picture

1. Click the Start button, point to Programs and then Accessories, and choose Paint.

2. Click a drawing tool.

3. Click the color you want to use.

4. Click an option for the selected tool.

5. Click to start the drawing.

6. Drag the end or corner of the shape and drop it to get the shape you want.

7. Keep choosing appropriate tools, colors, and options to complete your picture.

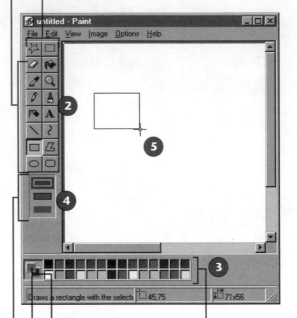

Paint's drawing tools

The Select tools

Sample of background color
Sample of foreground color
Options for selected tool

Color palette: right-click a color to change background color; left-click to change foreground color.

TIP

Bitmaps or Drawings?

A bitmap is a picture in which each line, circle, or shape is an integrated part of the picture— just like a picture drawn on paper. A drawing is a picture in which each line, circle, or shape is treated as an individually drawn object—like a collage assembled with cutout shapes. The Paint program creates bitmaps and is nice because of its simplicity. Drawing programs are useful for complex drawings and for pictures that need extensive editing.

TIP

Bitmap documents can be quite large. You can limit their size by saving the file at the lowest color depth that doesn't compromise the picture's quality. Unless it is a very high quality image, a 256-color bitmap is usually sufficient.

SEE ALSO

"Resize a Picture" on page 63 for information about resizing a picture.

Modify the Picture

1 Use one of the Select tools to select the part of the picture you want to work on. The illustration at the right shows a few examples of what you can do.

2 Use the Eraser tool to replace all colors with the background color.

Drag a handle... ...to resize the selection.

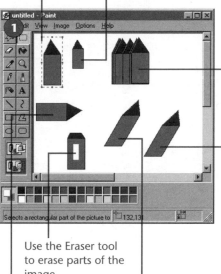

Hold down the Shift key and drag the selection to create a series of copies.

Hold down the Ctrl key, drag the selection, and drop a copy.

Use the Eraser tool to erase parts of the image.

Choose a command from the Image menu to rotate the selection... ...or to stretch and skew it.

4

Add Text to the Picture

1 Click the Text tool.

2 Drag out a text box for the text.

3 Choose the font, font size, and any emphasis you want to apply.

4 Type the text, and then click outside the text box to deselect it. Save the picture.

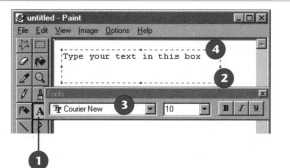

Editing a Picture

It's easy and fun to modify an existing bitmap picture to customize it, or to create a new picture using only part of the original picture. However, the picture must be a bitmap; if it isn't, you'll need a different program (rather than Paint) in which to edit it.

TIP

To replace one color with another, set the foreground color to the color to be replaced and the background color to the replacement color. Select the Eraser tool, and then hold down the right mouse button and drag the Eraser over the area where you want to replace the color.

TIP

If you don't see a thumbnail version of your picture, choose Zoom from the View menu, and then choose Show Thumbnail.

Edit a Picture

1 Start Paint if it isn't already running.

2 Choose Open from the File menu, locate the bitmap picture to be edited, and click Open.

3 Use the drawing tools to edit the picture.

4 Use the Magnifier tool to magnify the details so that you can fine-tune your edits; click the tool again to restore the view to normal size.

5 Save the picture.

6 If you want to rename the file, choose Save As from the File menu and type a new name for the picture.

Use the Magnifier tool.

Thumbnail shows context for the magnified area.

Select the level of magnification.

SEE ALSO

"Editing Inserted Material" on page 49 for information about editing a picture that is contained in another document.

Save a Portion of a Picture

1. Open the picture in Paint.

2. Use one of the Select tools to select the area to be saved.

3. Choose Copy To from the Edit menu.

4. In the Copy To dialog box, open the folder that will contain the picture, type a filename, and select the type of bitmap to be used.

Copy the selection to a new document.

TRY THIS

Not So Opaque. *Click the Opaque Paste option and paste a picture into a document. With the inserted picture still selected, right-click the color in the color palette that is used as the background for the inserted picture. With the inserted picture still selected, click the Paste Transparent option.*

Add a Picture to Another Picture

1. Open the picture that is to include another picture.

2. Click one of the Select tools.

3. Click Opaque Paste or Transparent Paste.

4. Choose Paste From from the Edit menu.

5. Locate the picture to be copied, and click Open.

6. Drag the pasted picture and drop it where you want it. Click outside the selection to deselect the pasted picture.

Drop the pasted picture where you want it.

Transparent Paste

Use Opaque Paste to include the pasted picture's background.

Creating Your Own Desktop Wallpaper

If you'd like to create your own Desktop wallpaper rather than using one of the ready-made patterns that come with Windows, you can use Paint to develop a design that expresses your personality or your mood of the day.

SEE ALSO

"Changing the Look of the Desktop" on page 126 for information about using the patterns and pictures that come with Windows.

"Making More Room on the Desktop" on page 129 for information about setting screen resolution.

Create Your Desktop Wallpaper

1 Start Paint.

2 Choose Attributes from the Image menu, and specify Width and Height.

3 Draw and save your picture.

4 Choose one of the Set As Wallpaper commands from the File menu:

- ◆ Choose Centered for a single full-screen picture.

- ◆ Choose Tiled for multiple instances of the same picture.

Set the values equal to your screen resolution for a single full-screen picture, or set them to a small value for the tiled wallpaper.

Viewing a Document Quickly

You can view the contents of many different types of documents to verify that you've found the document you're looking for, and you can do so without spending the time it takes to start the document's program. Quick View lives up to its name!

SEE ALSO

"Adding or Removing Windows Components" on page 156 for information about installing Quick View.

TIP

If you've installed a viewer for a specific program—Microsoft Word Viewer, for example— that viewer will be listed on a shortcut menu instead of Quick View. This type of program-specific viewer has more capabilities than Quick View and also has the ability to print a document.

View a Document

1. Right-click the document you want to view.

2. Choose Quick View from the shortcut menu.

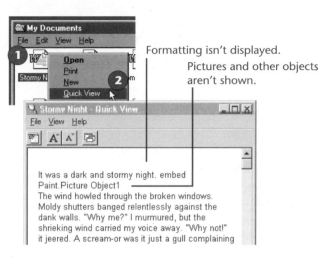

Formatting isn't displayed.

Pictures and other objects aren't shown.

View and Open a Different Document

1. Drag the document icon and drop it in the Quick View window to display the document.

2. Choose Open File For Editing from the File menu to open the document in its source program.

Click to open the document for editing.

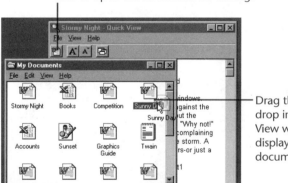

Drag the icon and drop in the Quick View window to display the document.

Printing a Document Without Opening It

If you want to print a document that is associated with a program—a Word document, for example—you can print it directly without starting the program. This doesn't mean that you don't need the program—it is still required for printing, but Windows will take care of all the details for you.

Print a Document Using the Default Printer

1 Select the document(s) to be printed.

2 Right-click a selected document, and choose Print from the shortcut menu.

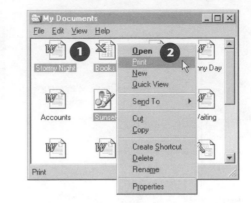

Print a Document Using a Specific Printer

1 Click the Start button, point to Settings, and choose Printers to open the Printers folder.

2 Select the document(s) to be printed.

3 Drag the selected document(s) to the Printers folder and drop on the printer you want to use.

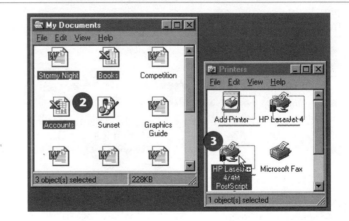

Quitting When You're Stuck

If a program isn't working properly but doesn't respond when you try to close it, Windows gives you an alternative course of action, which is known as "ending the task."

End the Task

1 Press Alt+Ctrl+Delete to display the Close Program dialog box.

2 Select the program that's misbehaving

3 Click the End Task button.

4 If Windows asks you whether you want to wait or end the task, click the End Task button.

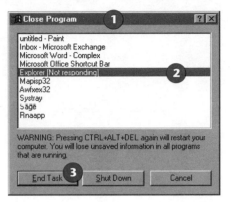

Take Drastic Steps

1 If the program will not close, close all other running programs.

2 Shut down Windows.

3 If Windows refuses to shut down, press Alt+Ctrl+Delete twice.

4 If Windows still refuses to shut down, turn off your computer.

4

5

Working with Multimedia

Multimedia! Depending on what you use your computer for, multimedia can mean work or play—or a little or a lot of each. If you're set up to work with multimedia on your computer—if, that is, you have a sound card installed, speakers or a headset, a CD-ROM drive, and, optionally, a microphone—Windows 95 is set to work with you.

You can play and create sounds, view video clips, and even play music CDs while you work. You can associate sounds with events that take place on your computer: if you'd like to hear a duck quacking every time you receive new mail, or your child's voice babbling baby language when you shut down your computer, you can make it so.

You can insert music clips into your dissertation on Beethoven or Brubeck; you can include video clips of your daughter's June wedding in your e-mail to a distant relative. Provided the person on the receiving end has a similarly equipped computer, the creative possibilities are endless. And, of course, multimedia opens up a whole new realm of wonderful educational and recreational tools—multimedia encyclopedias and other reference works; foreign-language courses; cooking and gardening programs; about a zillion exciting games…

Whether you use Windows multimedia features for work or for play, you're going to have a lot of fun.

Playing a Wave Sound

Windows works primarily with two different types of sounds: wave sounds, which are digital recordings of sounds, and MIDI (Musical Instrument Digital Interface) sequences.

SEE ALSO

"Playing a MIDI Sequence" on the facing page for information about MIDI sounds.

"Controlling the Sound Volume" on page 87 for information about changing sound levels.

TIP

If the Sound Recorder closes before you can make any changes, click the Start button, point your way through Programs, Accessories, and Multimedia, and then choose Sound Recorder.

Play a Sound

1 Open the folder containing the sound.

2 Double-click the sound file. The Sound Recorder opens, plays the sound, and closes when finished.

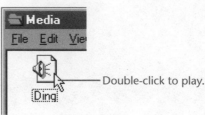

Double-click to play.

Control the Playback

1 While the sound is playing, click any of the control buttons, or use the slider.

2 Choose any of the playback effects from the Effects menu:

- Increase or decrease volume.
- Increase or decrease speed.
- Add an echo.
- Reverse the playback.

3 Close the program when you've finished.

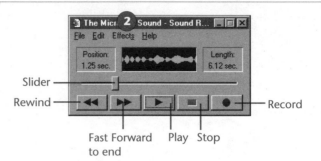

Slider

Rewind

Fast Forward to end

Play Stop

Record

Playing a MIDI Sequence

A MIDI sequence contains instructions (which could be compared to sheet music) that tell your sound card how to synthesize the music.

SEE ALSO

"Playing a Wave Sound" on the facing page for information about playing wave sounds.

"Controlling the Sound Volume" on page 87 for information about changing sound levels.

TIP

Most—but not all—sound cards support MIDI playback. If you can't play a MIDI sequence, read your sound-card documentation.

Play a Tune

1 Open the folder containing the MIDI file.

2 Double-click the file. Media Player opens, plays the file, and closes when finished.

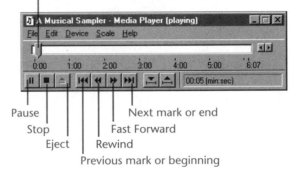
Double-click to play.

Control the Playback

1 Click any of the control buttons, or use the slider.

2 Close the program when you've finished.

Drag slider and drop to play a different part.

Pause
Stop
Eject
Previous mark or beginning
Rewind
Fast Forward
Next mark or end

Playing a Video Clip

Most videos are played as part of a program and their playing is controlled by the program. You can, however, play a video directly using Media Player.

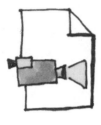

TIP

It's tempting to set your video to play in a full screen, but be aware that many videos are very grainy at that size. Experiment to find the best setting for a video on your display.

Set the Size of Video Playback

1. Click the Start button, point to Settings, and choose Control Panel.

2. Double-click Multimedia.

3. Click the Video tab.

4. Select the size of the playback.

5. Click OK.

Play a Video Clip

Double-click the video file. Media Player opens, plays the video, and closes when finished.

Multimedia

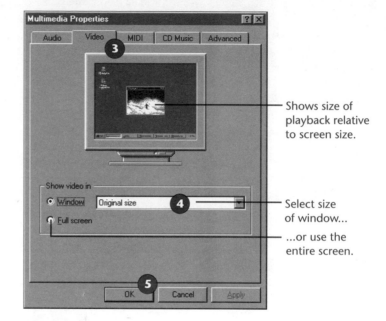

Shows size of playback relative to screen size.

Select size of window...

...or use the entire screen.

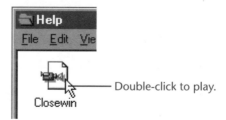

Double-click to play.

TIP

Windows 95 has Video For Windows built in, so you can play AVI-type videos. To be able to play other video formats, such as MPEG, you'll need additional software and the appropriate hardware configuration.

TIP

Most—but not all—videos include sound. Make sure you have a sound card and speakers installed to get the most from your videos.

SEE ALSO

"Controlling the Sound Volume" on page 87 for information about changing sound levels.

Control the Playback

1. Click any of the control buttons, or use the slider. If the video is full screen, click the video to reveal the controls.

2. Close the window when you've finished.

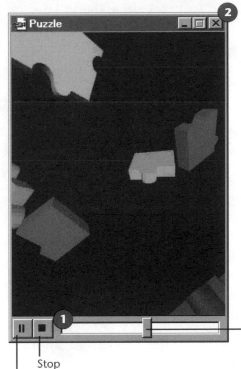

Drag slider and drop to change position in file.

Stop

Pause (changes to Play when stopped)

5

Creating a Sound File

If you have a microphone—also called an *external input device*—you can create your own sound files. Even without an external input device, you can create your own sound files by combining and editing your existing sound files.

Set Up a Sound File

1. Open the folder that will contain the sound file.

2. Right-click, point to New, and choose Wave Sound from the shortcut menu.

3. Type a name for the sound file, and press Enter.

4. Double-click the file to start Sound Recorder.

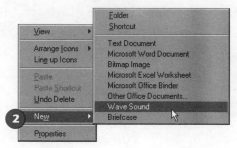

Set Options

1. Choose Audio Properties from the Edit menu.

2. Choose the settings for your recording.

3. Click OK.

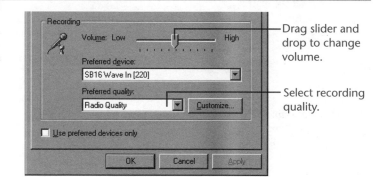

Drag slider and drop to change volume.

Select recording quality.

Record Sounds

1. Click the Record button.

2. Speak, sing, whistle, or otherwise make sounds in front of the microphone.

3. Click Stop when you've finished.

4. Choose Save from the File menu.

Add Sounds and Effects

1. Move the slider to the location in the sound file where you want to add an existing sound file.

2. From the Edit menu, choose

    ◆ Insert File to add a file and record over any existing sound.

    ◆ Mix With File to merge a file with the existing sound.

3. Locate the file and click Open.

4. Choose the type of effect you want to add from the Effects menu.

Each click increases or decreases speed.

Click once for new echo.

Each click increases or decreases volume.

5

Associating a Sound with an Event

If you want audio cues for events in Windows—closing a program or receiving new mail, for example—you can assign wave sounds to these events.

Qhack!

SEE ALSO

"Controlling the Sound Volume" on page 87 for information about changing sound levels.

"Switching Desktop Themes" on page 263 for information about the sound schemes available with Microsoft Plus!

TIP

Put any sound files that you want to use for events in the Media folder (in the Windows folder), and the sounds will appear in the Name list.

Assign a Sound to an Event

1 Click the Start button, point to Settings, and choose Control Panel from the submenu.

2 Double-click Sounds.

3 Select an event from the Events list.

4 Select a sound from the Name list, or use the Browse button to find a sound in another folder.

5 Save the sound scheme after assigning it.

6 Click OK when you've finished.

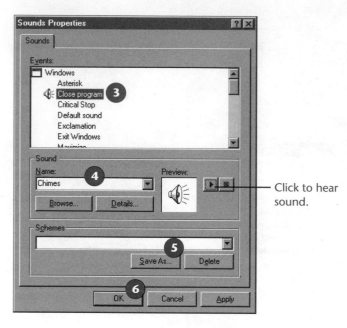

Click to hear sound.

Playing a Music CD

You can just drop a music CD into your disc drive and play it, or you can use CD Player to control how the CD is played.

SEE ALSO

"Creating a CD Play List" on page 86 for information about programming CD Player.

"Controlling the Sound Volume" on page 87 for information about changing sound levels.

TIP

If the CD doesn't start automatically, click the Start button, point your way through Programs, Accessories, and Multimedia, and then choose CD Player from the submenu.

TIP

Choose Preferences from the Options menu to set how long each track is played when using Intro Play.

Play a CD

1. Insert the CD into the disc drive.

2. Wait for Windows to start playing the disc.

3. Listen and enjoy!

4. Click the CD Player button on the taskbar.

5. Choose any play options from the Options menu to modify the way the music is played.

   ◆ Random Order to have CD Player decide the order in which the tracks are played.

   ◆ Continuous Play to resume playing the CD after the last track has been played.

   ◆ Intro Play to play the first few seconds of each track.

6. Click any control button, or choose a new option from the Artist or Track drop-down list box.

Switch to different CD drive.   Play   Pause

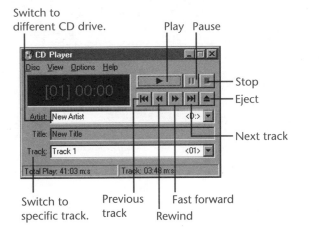

Stop
Eject
Next track

Switch to specific track.   Previous track   Rewind   Fast forward

Creating a CD Play List

By creating a play list, you can program which tracks are played and what order they're played in. You can create a play list for each CD and save the list. Then, whenever that CD is loaded, Windows will use the play list.

SEE ALSO

"Playing a Music CD" on page 85 for information about using CD Player.

TIP

Create a Mood. *If you want to play only a few tracks, click Clear All, and then add the tracks from the Available Tracks list.*

Define a CD

1 Insert the CD into the disc drive and click the CD Player button on the taskbar.

2 Choose Edit Play List from the Disc menu.

3 Type the name of the recording artist.

4 Type the name of the CD.

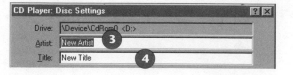

Create a Play List

Create your own concert:

- ◆ Remove unwanted tracks from the play list.

- ◆ Change the order of play.

- ◆ Name the tracks for easy identification.

Drag the track and drop it at a new location.

4

Select a track whose position you want to change.
3

Click Remove.
2

CD Player: Disc Settings

Drive: \Device\CdRom0 <D:>
Artist: New Artist
Title: New Title

Play List:
- Very Cool
- Ultra Cool
- Cool
- Track 4
- Track 5
- Track 6
- Track 7
- Track 8
- Track 9

<-- Add
Remove ->
Clear All
Reset

Available Tracks:
- Very Cool
- Ultra Cool
- Cool
- Track 4
- Track 5
- Track 6
- Track 7
- Track 8
- Track 9
- Track 10

5 Select a track to name.

Track 04: Track 4
Set Name **7** Click to set the name.

OK   Cancel

1 Select a track you want to remove from the list.

8 Click when finished.

6 Type a name for the track.

Controlling the Sound Volume

You can keep your music and other sounds muted so that you don't disturb other people, or, when you're the only person around, you can crank the sound level up and blast away! Although many programs have individual controls, you can use the volume control to set all your sound levels.

TIP

If the Volume icon doesn't appear on the taskbar, open Multimedia Properties from the Control Panel and, on the Audio tab, turn on the Show Volume Control On The Taskbar check box.

TIP

Many speakers have built-in volume controls. You can use these in conjunction with the volume control on the taskbar to fine-tune your sound levels.

Set the Master Volume Level

1 Click the Volume icon on the taskbar.

2 Drag the slider and drop it to adjust the volume.

3 Click outside the Volume icon to close it.

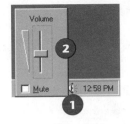

Set the Volume for Individual Devices

1 Double-click the Volume icon on the taskbar.

2 Adjust the settings for your devices.

Master control affects all devices.

Drag slider and drop to adjust balance.

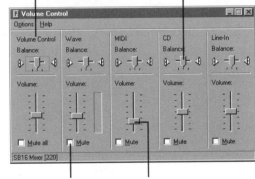

Check for no sound.

Drag slider and drop to change volume.

5

Inserting Part of a Multimedia File into a Document

You can use Media Player to insert a section of a wave sound, MIDI sequence, or video-clip file into a program. Although only part of the file will play from the document, the entire multimedia file must be available to the document.

SEE ALSO

"Copying Material Between Documents" on page 48 for information about copying items from one document to another.

Get the File

1. Click the Start button, point to Programs, Accessories, and Multimedia, and then choose Media Player.

2. Choose the type of multimedia file to be used from the Device menu.

3. Locate and select the file, and click OK.

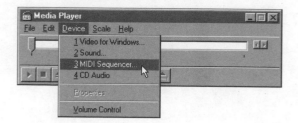

Define and Copy a Section

1. Drag the slider and drop it at the beginning of the section to be copied.

2. Click the Start Selection button.

3. Drag the slider and drop it at the end of the section to be copied.

4. Click the End Selection button.

5. Choose Options from the Edit menu and set the options.

6. Choose Copy Object from the Edit menu.

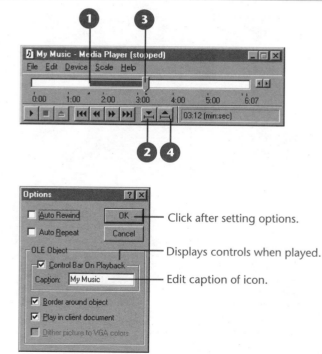

— Click after setting options.

— Displays controls when played.

— Edit caption of icon.

Add a Soundtrack. *Find a MIDI file you like. Open a document and add sound clips from selected areas of the document using Media Player.*

If you're sending a video file or a MIDI file by e-mail, send the entire file rather than part of it; otherwise, the recipient won't be able to play it. To create a new file that contains only part of the original video file or MIDI file, use one of the many excellent programs available for editing videos or MIDI music.

To create a new sound file with only part of the original file, use Sound Recorder to delete the parts you don't want to keep, and save the part you do want as a new file.

Insert the Section

1. Switch to the document that is to contain the multimedia section.

2. Click to place the insertion point where you want the multimedia section.

3. Choose Paste from the Edit menu. (If the receiving program doesn't have a Paste command, or if the Paste command is grayed and unavailable, the program is probably unable to include multimedia files.)

4. Save the document.

5. Double-click the inserted multimedia item to verify that it plays correctly.

5

6

Using Windows System Tools

Like your house, your car, your garden—and yes, even you yourself—your computer can benefit from a little preventive medicine here, a little diagnosis, tune-up, and maintenance there. We're not suggesting that you take your computer apart and try and put it back together again; if things go *really* haywire, bring in the experts! But Windows does provide a suite of easy-to-use tools that can help you tune up your computer and get it running at top speed.

Should you be struck by a virus, a corrupted hard disk, or a similar misfortune, you can guard against the loss of hours of work by *backing up*—that is, copying—your system using the Backup tool, and then consistently backing up all new and changed work. That's the preventive part.

You can find and fix disk errors using the ScanDisk tool to give your hard disk a regularly scheduled "physical." That's the diagnosis and maintenance part.

You can speed up the time it takes to access your files using the Disk Defragmenter tool, and you can even double your disk space using the DriveSpace tool. That's the tune-up part.

This section gives you just a brief tour of the system tools, but as you use them you'll find helpful, step-by-step onscreen instructions to guide you.

Backing Up Your System

You can back up all the files on your hard disk, including your system settings, to a tape drive, to disks, or to a network share. With your system backed up, you can easily restore any or all files should disaster strike. The backed-up files are stored in a special compressed format, and you can retrieve the information by using Backup again. If you're going to back up to a network server, see your system administrator for instructions on using network backup tools.

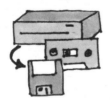

Start the Backup Program

1. Click the Start button, point to Programs, Accessories, and System Tools, and choose Backup from the submenu.

2. If a welcome window appears, read the details and click OK.

3. If a message appears informing you that a Full System Backup file set has been created, read the details and click OK.

Start the System Backup

1. In the Backup window, choose Open File Set from the File menu.

2. Select Full System Backup if it's not already listed in the File Name box, and click Open.

3. Wait while Backup makes a copy of the computer's settings and selects the files to be copied.

4. Click the Next Step button.

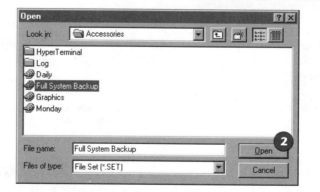

Create a Backup File

1. Select the device or location for the backed-up file set.

2. Click Start Backup.

3. Type a name for the file set.

4. Click OK.

5. WAIT—this could take a long time.

6. Click OK when Windows tells you that the backup is complete.

7. Close the Backup window.

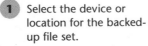

Backing Up Your Most Recent Work

We've all heard "It's not *if* you're going to lose files, but *when.*" Most of us ignored this weary phrase until its prophecy came to pass, we lost valuable information, and then...*we understood!* To minimize the impact, back up your changed files to tape, disks, or a network share on a periodic basis. The first time you run it, Backup takes quite a long time to back up all your files, but subsequent backups are much quicker because it's only your changed files that are being backed up.

Select What You Want to Back Up

1. Start the Backup program by clicking the Start button, pointing to Programs, Accessories, and System Tools, and choosing Backup from the submenu.

2. If a welcome window appears, read the details and click OK.

3. Select the drive or folders to be backed up.

4. Choose Options from the Settings menu.

5. Select the Incremental option on the Backup tab, and click OK.

6. Click Next Step.

Grayed check box indicates that some folders and files are selected.

Check mark indicates that all files in folder are selected.

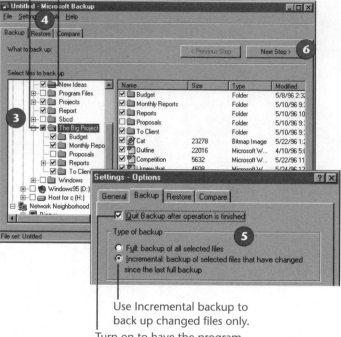

Use Incremental backup to back up changed files only.

Turn on to have the program close after backup is completed.

TIP

Drag the Backup icon onto the Windows Desktop for easy access (and as a reminder to back up your files).

TIP

Set up a backup schedule based on the amount of work you do and how invaluable your work is. A popular and practical routine is to conduct an incremental backup daily, a full backup of all your work folders weekly, and a full system backup monthly.

Create the Backup

1. Select the destination device or location for the backup.

2. Choose Save from the File menu.

3. Enter a name for the backup, and click OK.

4. Click Start Backup.

5. Type a name for the file set, and click OK.

6. WAIT—this might take a while.

7. Click OK when Windows tells you that the backup is complete.

8. Close the Backup window.

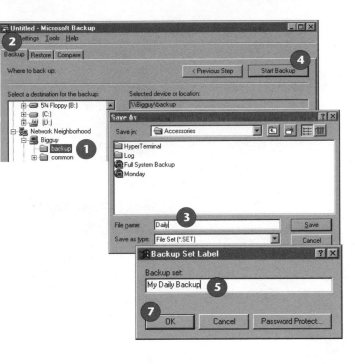

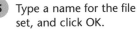

Back Up Files Routinely

1. Open My Computer, open the Program Files folder, and then open the Accessories folder.

2. Double-click the backed-up file-set icon.

3. Click Yes.

4. Wait for the files to be selected and for your new or changed files to be backed up.

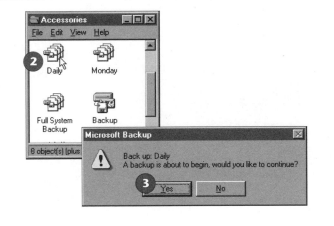

6

Retrieving Backed-Up Files

Whether you've backed up a few files or your entire system, you can retrieve the information using the Backup program.

TIP

It's Here Somewhere! *If you don't remember which file set contains the file or files you want to restore, select a file set and click the Next Step button to explore the contents. If what you're looking for isn't there, click the Previous Step button and select another file set.*

SEE ALSO

"Backing Up Your Most Recent Work" on page 94 for information about backing up your files.

Open the Backup File

1. Start the Backup program.
2. Click the Restore tab.
3. Locate and select the file set to be restored.
4. Click the Next Step button.

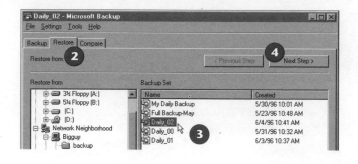

Select What You Want to Restore

1. Select the folders and files to be restored.
2. Click Start Restore.
3. Click OK when Windows tells you that the files have been restored.
4. Close the Backup window.

Click to check and restore all backed-up files.

Click to check and restore all backed-up files in the folder...

...or open a folder...

...and select individual files to restore.

Improving Disk Performance

When Windows stores a file on your hard disk, the file contents are often broken down into small pieces and stored wherever there's available space. Over time, what with the other files you've added or deleted, these file fragments can get scattered all over your disk. So, when you want a particular file, Windows has to wander around the disk, finding and gathering up the pieces. To decrease the time you spend drumming your fingers on the desk, you can use Disk Defragmenter to bring the pieces of the file together and thus speed up the time your computer takes to access files.

> **TIP**
>
> **Hands Off!** *Leave your computer alone when Disk Defragmenter is running. Any change to the disk contents causes the program to restart the defragmentation process.*

Run Disk Defragmenter

1 Click the Start button, point to Programs, Accessories, and System Tools, and choose Disk Defragmenter from the submenu.

2 Select the drive to be defragmented, and click OK.

3 Click Start.

4 Wait.

5 Click Yes to quit or No to defragment another drive.

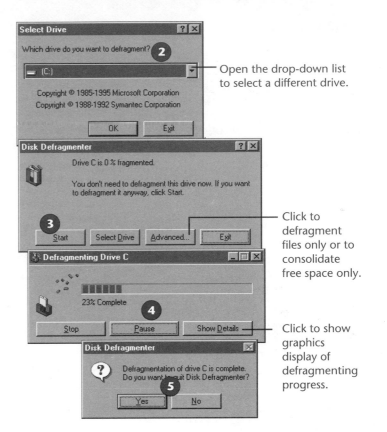

Open the drop-down list to select a different drive.

Click to defragment files only or to consolidate free space only.

Click to show graphics display of defragmenting progress.

6

Finding and Fixing Disk Errors

Sometimes, as the result of programs that misbehave or some other anomaly, your computer can lose track of a file or parts of a file. These disconnected bits and pieces occupy valuable space on your hard disk. You can use ScanDisk to check your disk, find these sections, and recover them if they contain valuable lost information. Otherwise, you can delete them to free up space on your hard disk.

TIP

Recovered file segments are stored in the disk's root directory as .CHK files. Open the file as a text document and see if there's anything you want to save.

SEE ALSO

"Running Automatic Maintenance" on pages 260–261 for information about running ScanDisk automatically.

Run ScanDisk

1. Click the Start button, point to Programs, Accessories, and System Tools, and choose ScanDisk from the submenu.

2. Select the drive that you want checked.

3. Select the type of test.

4. Turn on the option to fix errors automatically.

5. Click Start.

6. After the test is complete, read the statistics, and then click OK.

7. Close ScanDisk.

Run a Standard test most of the time.
Run a Thorough test periodically to also check the physical surface of the hard disk for any bad spots.

Creating Additional Disk Space

When disk space is at a premium, you can compress files by compressing the disk drive with DriveSpace. The good news: compressing a drive increases disk space by 50 to 100 percent! The bad news: the procedure can take hours, and, unfortunately, you have to answer some questions along the way, so you can't just start the process and go out to a movie.

TIP

DriveSpace can create a compressed drive of up to 512 MB; any additional space will not be compressed.

SEE ALSO

"Backing Up Your Most Recent Work" on page 94 for information about backing up files.

Compress Your Drive

1 Click the Start button, point to Programs, Accessories, and System Tools, and choose DriveSpace from the submenu.

2 Select the drive to be compressed.

3 Choose Compress from the Drive menu.

4 Click Start.

5 Back up your files if you haven't already done so.

6 Start the compression.

7 Click OK when Windows tells you to restart the computer.

8 Click OK when Windows tells you that DriveSpace has finished. DriveSpace creates an additional drive, usually drive H. Ignore this drive—it's created solely so that DriveSpace can administer compression.

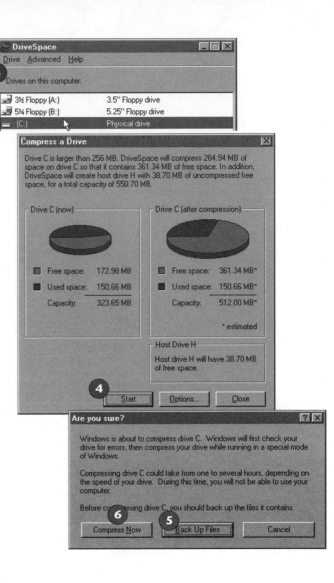

Running MS-DOS

7

Using Microsoft Windows 95 doesn't mean that you have to abandon your MS-DOS–based programs. Most of them run extremely well in Windows 95, some can be tricked into running in Windows, and the few that don't work in Windows can usually be run in an exclusive MS-DOS mode.

Earlier versions of Windows "sat on top of" MS-DOS, and the two systems were essentially separate operating systems. MS-DOS is now part of the Windows operating system, giving you the best of both worlds. You can work at the MS-DOS prompt if that's your favorite way to work. You can run your old—and new—MS-DOS–based games. Or you can switch back and forth between MS-DOS and Windows as needed.

We'll cover some of the basic tasks here: starting MS-DOS–based programs, working from the command line, moving or copying text between Windows and MS-DOS, running in MS-DOS mode only, and generally making MS-DOS–based programs perform at their top level. We'll even show you a way to trick a bratty and selfish MS-DOS program into thinking that Windows isn't running and that it has the entire system to itself.

Our goal in this section is to help you get the most from your MS-DOS–based programs, whether you use them for work or for play.

Running MS-DOS Commands

If you need to work from the MS-DOS prompt, you can open an MS-DOS window and execute all your MS-DOS activities there, including using the basic MS-DOS commands, starting a program from the MS-DOS prompt, and even starting a program in a new window.

SEE ALSO

"Managing a Program Window" on page 12 for information about working with program windows, and "Arranging Windows on the Desktop" on page 28 for information about arranging your open program windows.

Open an MS-DOS Window

1 Click the Start button, point to Programs, and choose MS-DOS Prompt from the submenu.

2 If the toolbar isn't visible, click the MS-DOS icon and choose Toolbar from the menu.

3 Customize the window to your liking:

◆ Change the font size in the Font drop-down list. The window will resize to accommodate the new font size.

◆ Click the Full Screen button on the toolbar if you want the window to fill the entire screen. Hold down the Alt key and press Enter to return the window to its original size.

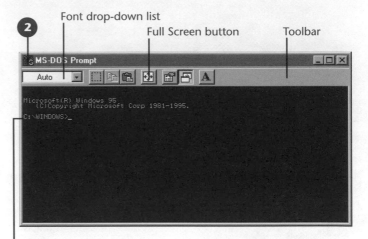

Font drop-down list
Full Screen button
Toolbar

MS-DOS prompt

Try typing these MS-DOS commands, and see how switches after each command affect the results.

Type cd \Windows *and press Enter*

Type Mem *and press Enter*

Type Mem /c/p *and press Enter*

Type Dir *and press Enter*

Type Dir /w *and press Enter*

Type Dir /? *and press Enter to see the different ways to run a command.*

Changes you make to the environment with commands such as Path and Prompt affect the current MS-DOS session only. To make these changes permanent, edit the Autoexec.bat file to include these settings.

Enter an MS-DOS Command

Do any of the following at the prompt:

- Type an MS-DOS command, and press Enter.

- Type an MS-DOS command with additional information or switches to modify the command, and press Enter.

- Type Exit, and press Enter to end the MS-DOS session and close the MS-DOS Prompt window.

Type an MS-DOS command, and press Enter.

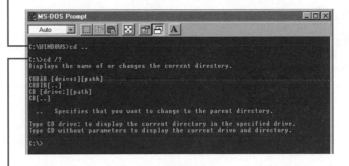

Type an MS-DOS command followed by a space, a slash, and a question mark to get help on the command.

TOP 10 MS-DOS COMMANDS	
Command	**What it does**
CD	Changes to the specified directory.
CLS	Clears the screen.
Copy	Copies the specified files or folders.
Dir	Shows contents of the current directory.
[*Drive letter:*]	Changes to the specified drive (type drive letter and colon).
Exit	Ends the MS-DOS session.
Mem	Displays memory configuration.
Path	Displays or sets the path MS-DOS searches.
Prompt	Changes the information displayed at the prompt.
Rename	Renames the specified file.

Starting a Program from the MS-DOS Prompt

When you're working in an MS-DOS window, you can start an MS-DOS–based program in that window or in a new window. You can even start a Windows program from an MS-DOS window. If you don't remember the MS-DOS path and filename, you can find the program in Windows and then let Windows insert the information for you.

Start a Program

1 Open an MS-DOS window, type the program's path and filename, and press Enter.

2 When finished, use the program's menu to exit the program and return to the MS-DOS prompt.

Current directory
Path to subdirectory
Program filename

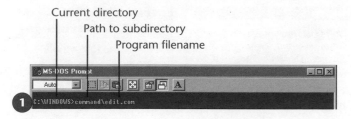

Find a Program to Run

1 Type *start* followed by a space and a period, and press Enter.

2 Navigate through the folders to find the program.

3 Arrange the windows so that the MS-DOS window and the program window are both visible.

4 Drag the program and drop it in the MS-DOS window.

5 Click in the MS-DOS window if it's not the active window, and press Enter to start the program. When you've finished, use the program's menu to exit the program and return to the MS-DOS prompt.

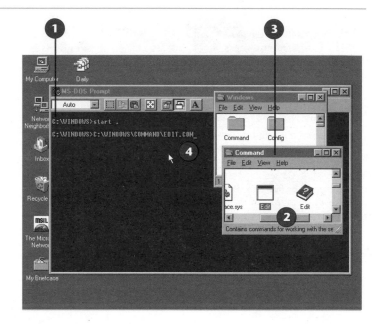

SEE ALSO

"Managing a Program Window" on page 12 for information about working with program windows, and "Arranging Windows on the Desktop" on page 28 for information about arranging your open program windows.

"Running MS-DOS Commands" on page 102 for information about opening a window and working at the MS-DOS prompt.

TRY THIS

At the MS-DOS prompt, use the CD command if necessary to switch to the Windows directory. Type dir *.exe /on/w *to list the programs in alphabetical order. At the prompt, type* start, *and then type the name of one of the listed programs. Don't start any programs you're unfamiliar with—some are pretty powerful—but try any of the following to access items that aren't on the Start menu:*

> *taskman.exe*
> *winfile.exe*
> *write.exe*
> *program.exe*

Close each program when you've finished with it.

Start an MS-DOS Program in a New Window

1 Type *start* at the beginning of the command line.

2 Type or drag and drop the program's path and filename, and press Enter.

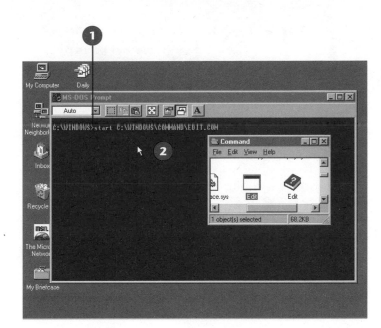

Start a Windows-Based Program

1 Type *start* at the beginning of the command line.

2 Type the name of the Windows-based program, and press Enter.

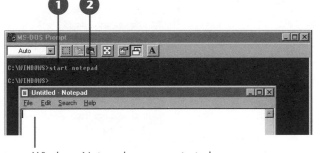

Windows Notepad program started from the MS-DOS command prompt

Copying Text in MS-DOS

Now that MS-DOS is part of Windows, the two systems interact even better than they did previously. You can easily share text between your MS-DOS output, the MS-DOS command line, any MS-DOS–based programs, and even your Windows-based programs.

SEE ALSO

"Copying Material Between Documents" on page 48 for information about copying and pasting text.

"Running MS-DOS Commands" on page 102 for information about working at the MS-DOS prompt.

Copy MS-DOS Output

1 Run your MS-DOS command in an MS-DOS window.

2 If the toolbar isn't visible, click the MS-DOS icon and choose Toolbar from the menu.

3 Click the Mark button.

4 Click to position the mouse pointer where you want to start the selection.

5 Hold down the left mouse button, drag over the area to be copied, and release the mouse button.

6 Click the Copy button.

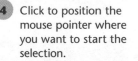

```
Select - MS-DOS Prompt
Auto

C:\WINDOWS\COMMAND>cd..

C:\WINDOWS>mem

Memory Type        Total        Used        Free
----------------   --------     --------    --------
Conventional          640K          35K        605K
Upper                   0K           0K          0K
Reserved              384K         384K          0K
Extended (XMS)     15,360K         156K     15,204K
----------------   --------     --------    --------
Total memory       16,384K         575K     15,809K

Total under 1 MB      640K          35K        605K

Total Expanded (EMS)                       16M (16,285,696 bytes)
Free Expanded (EMS)                        16M (16,285,696 bytes)

Largest executable program size       605K (619,008 bytes)
Largest free upper memory block         0K       (0 bytes)
MS-DOS is resident in the high memory area.

C:\WINDOWS>
```

Paste Text into a Windows-Based Program

1 Switch to the Windows-based program.

2 Choose Paste from the Edit menu.

```
Document - WordPad
File  Edit  View  Insert  Format  Help

Here is the information on the computer system that you
requested:

Memory Type        Total        Used        Free
----------------   --------     --------    --------
Conventional          640K          35K        605K
Upper                   0K           0K          0K
Reserved              384K         384K          0K
Extended (XMS)     15,360K         156K     15,204K
----------------   --------     --------    --------
Total memory       16,384K         575K     15,809K
```

Text from the MS-DOS window

SEE ALSO

"Managing Multiple Programs" on page 46 for information about switching between program windows.

TRY THIS

MS-DOS Quick Reference. *Create a document in WordPad and list the MS-DOS commands that you use frequently. Next to each command add an explanation of what it does. Save the document. When you're working in MS-DOS and can't remember the command you need, open the document, copy the command, switch back to your MS-DOS window, and paste the command into the command line.*

Copy Text from Windows into MS-DOS

1. Copy text from the Windows document.

2. Switch to the MS-DOS window.

3. Click the Paste button.

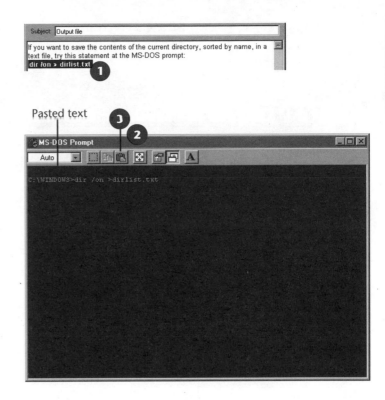

Pasted text

Starting an MS-DOS– Based Program from Windows

Windows is smart enough to recognize an MS-DOS–based program and to start an MS-DOS session for you when you start an MS-DOS–based program. After seeing how the program runs, you might want to customize the way it looks.

SEE ALSO

"Getting an MS-DOS Program to Run" on page 112 if you have any problems running a program.

Run a Program

1 Locate the program in its folder.

2 Double-click the program.

3 When finished, use the program's menu to exit. If the program terminated by itself but didn't close the MS-DOS window, click the Close button in the upper right corner of the window.

Double-click to run.

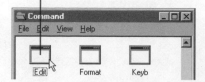

Choose to end the program and close the window.

Customize a Program's Appearance

1. Right-click the program icon and choose Properties from the shortcut menu.

2. Click the Program tab and set the size of the window.

3. Click the Font tab and select the font size you want to use.

4. Click the Screen tab, set the size of the program, and specify whether you want the toolbar to be displayed.

5. Click OK.

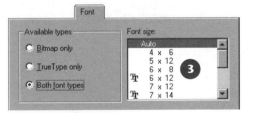

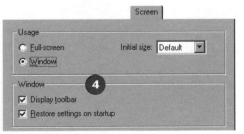

Navigating Folders in MS-DOS

Working in MS-DOS usually means working with paths and using the traditional MS-DOS filenames. But you can also use Windows folders and long filenames to help you navigate. Folders in the world of MS-DOS are called *directories*, and MS-DOS directory names are limited to eight characters in length, with an optional three-character extension.

TIP

To switch to a folder on a different drive, first switch to that drive by typing the drive letter followed by a colon at the command prompt, and press Enter. Then use the CD command to switch to the folder.

Switch Between Folders

Use any of the Change Directory (CD) commands shown in the table at the right. Substitute the actual paths and folder names for those shown here, and include the quotation marks where indicated.

MS-DOS COMMANDS FOR CHANGING FOLDERS	
Command	**What it does**
CD . .	Moves up one folder (to parent folder).
CD . . .	Moves up two folders.
CD	Moves up three folders.
CD *MS-DOS directory name*	Moves to specified subfolder.
CD *path**MS-DOS directory name*	Moves to specified folder.
CD *"long folder name"*	Moves to specified subfolder.
CD *path**"long folder name"*	Moves to specified folder.

Use a Folder Window

1. Type your command.

2. Switch to the folder window.

3. Drag the folder and drop it at the command prompt.

4. Press Enter.

Dropped folder shows full MS-DOS path.

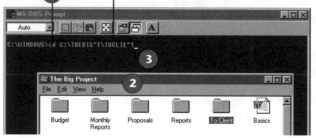

Running in MS-DOS Mode Only

You can start MS-DOS without starting Windows, or, if Windows is running, you can exit Windows and restart the computer in MS-DOS mode.

TIP

If you or any of your MS-DOS programs have made changes to the MS-DOS configuration, shut down your computer before restarting Windows to reset the original configuration settings.

SEE ALSO

"Running MS-DOS Commands" on page 102 for information about working at the MS-DOS prompt.

Start MS-DOS Without Starting Windows

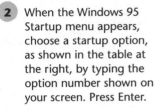

1. Start your computer. When you see the message "Starting Windows 95," press the F8 function key.

2. When the Windows 95 Startup menu appears, choose a startup option, as shown in the table at the right, by typing the option number shown on your screen. Press Enter.

3. Run your MS-DOS–based program.

4. Exit the program and turn your computer off. Turn your computer back on to start Windows.

End a Windows Session and Work in MS-DOS

1. Click the Start button, and choose Shut Down.

2. Click Restart The Computer In MS-DOS Mode.

3. Click Yes.

4. Work from the MS-DOS command line. When finished, turn off the computer, or type *win* to return to Windows.

WINDOWS 95 STARTUP OPTIONS	
Option	**What it does**
Command prompt only	Loads any startup files and displays MS-DOS prompt.
Safe Mode command prompt only	Bypasses startup files and displays MS-DOS prompt.
Previous version of MS-DOS	Loads any startup files and runs the version of MS-DOS that was installed before Windows was installed (provided you chose to keep the previous MS-DOS version during Windows Setup).

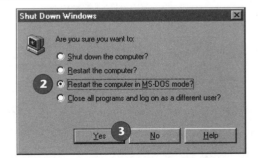

Getting an MS-DOS Program to Run

If an MS-DOS program won't run, you can adjust your system's settings to accommodate the program's needs. Some MS-DOS programs are unfriendly and refuse to run when Windows is running. Some are greedy and want a huge chunk of your computer's resources; others are just plain selfish and want the entire system to themselves. You might need to experiment a bit to find the technique that's exactly right for your program.

Change the Available Memory

1. Right-click the program icon and choose Properties from the shortcut menu.

2. Click the Memory tab and try new memory settings.

3. Click OK to close the program's Properties dialog box.

Set to program specifications.

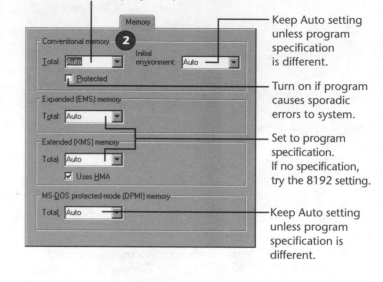

Keep Auto setting unless program specification is different.

Turn on if program causes sporadic errors to system.

Set to program specification. If no specification, try the 8192 setting.

Keep Auto setting unless program specification is different.

Pretend That Windows Isn't Running

1. Right-click the program icon and choose Properties. On the Program tab, click the Advanced button.

2. Turn on the Prevent MS-DOS–Based Programs From Detecting Windows option.

3. Click OK to close the Advanced Program Settings and click OK to close the program's Properties dialog box.

Turn on to make your program think that Windows isn't running.

7

TIP

When your computer is running in MS-DOS mode, Windows restarts when you close the MS-DOS program.

SEE ALSO

Section 15, "Taking Care of Problems," starting on page 275, for information about getting advice on problems in specific programs.

TIP

Most companies that develop programs have Web sites. Check their pages for tips on getting the most from your programs.

TIP

Dead End! *A few old MS-DOS programs simply will not run with the version of MS-DOS that is part of Windows 95, and some won't run if your computer has a Pentium processor. This is usually due to special programming techniques that no longer work with the newer versions of MS-DOS or with newer hardware.*

Run in MS-DOS Mode Only

1. Right-click the program icon and choose Properties from the shortcut menu.

2. On the Program tab, click the Advanced button.

3. Turn on the MS-DOS Mode option.

4. Change other settings as needed.

5. Click OK to close the Advanced Program Settings dialog box.

6. Click OK to close the program's Properties dialog box.

Closes all programs and runs only in MS-DOS mode.

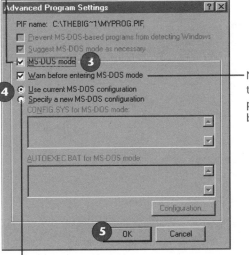

Notifies you that all Windows programs will be closed.

Select only if program specification requires special Config.sys and Autoexec.bat settings.

Customizing Your Computer

Most of us tend to choose our clothes, our furniture, and the various other trappings of our daily lives based on personal preferences that include style, size, color, comfort, and efficiency. You love your old car because you're tall and it has enough headroom; I love my blue suede shoes because they're...blue. These preferences are part of our personalities—they might change radically over time but, for better or worse, we always have at least a few of them.

Now that computers are a part of so many people's daily lives, we want our computers to reflect our personalities, too. Whether it's your own computer or your employer's, and whether you're the only person who uses it or one of several users, you can customize your computer so that it looks and works exactly the way you want it to. You can change the size and color of almost everything, and you can make adjustments to the ways in which various features work so that you can get your work done faster and more easily. If you do share your computer with other people, each of you can set up your own customization and do your work in your chosen environment.

Microsoft Windows 95 makes it easy and fun to customize your computer, whether you do it one time only or once a month.

Setting Up a Computer for Different Users

Windows remembers. If you share your computer with other people—or even if you don't—you can tell Windows how you want the computer set up. Then, every time you log on, Windows will set up your preferences, or your *user profile.* You can do the same thing if you work on a network, too, so that when you log on to any network computer with Windows 95, your preferences will be set up on that computer.

Create a User Profile

1 Click the Start button, point to Settings, and choose Control Panel from the submenu.

2 Double-click the Passwords icon.

3 Click the User Profiles tab.

4 Click the option that lets you customize your settings.

5 Turn the appropriate options on or off to define what Windows remembers.

6 Click OK.

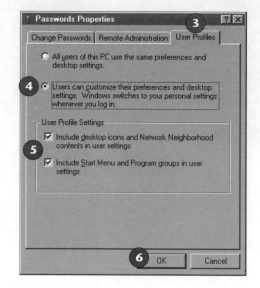

Sweeten the Deal. *Your system administrator can override any of your settings and lock you out of some options. If you can't set your own preferences, bring your system administrator some cookies and ask for full access to your profile.*

You can create more than one profile for yourself if you want. If, for example, you use your computer at different times for very different types of tasks, you can set up a separate profile, using a different name, for each task session. When you log on under each name, all the tools you need for that particular type of task will be set up exactly as you need them. If you're connected to a network, you'll need to log on to the network separately so that you're using the correct network user name.

Save Your Settings

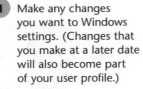

1 Make any changes you want to Windows settings. (Changes that you make at a later date will also become part of your user profile.)

2 Click the Start button and choose Shut Down.

3 Select the Restart The Computer option, and click OK to save your settings.

4 Log on with your user name.

EXAMPLES OF WHAT YOU CAN CUSTOMIZE	
Item	**Example**
Desktop icons	Add a shortcut to a program.
Start menu	Remove a program that you never use.
Windows taskbar	Move the taskbar to a new location.
Network connections	Map a drive to a network resource.
Screen appearance	Change screen colors.
Sounds	Choose a new sound scheme.
Multimedia	Play video full screen.
Keyboard	Use a different-language keyboard.
Regional settings	Use a different decimal separator.
Mouse	Change the pointers.
My Computer	Display the MS-DOS path in the title bar.

8

Customizing the Taskbar

The taskbar is a really great tool for switching quickly back and forth between programs. If you want, you can alter it so that it's even better suited to your working style. You can park it at any of the four sides of your screen, change its size, and even make it disappear when you don't need it and reappear when you do.

Move the Taskbar

1 Point to an empty part of the taskbar.

2 Drag the taskbar and drop it at the top, bottom, or either side of your screen.

Drop the taskbar at any edge of the screen.

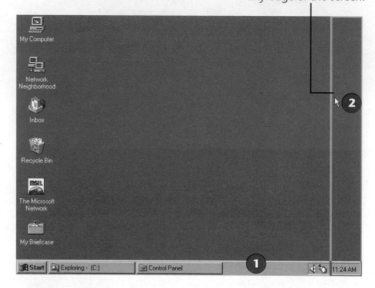

Resize the Taskbar

1 Move the pointer over the inside edge of the taskbar until the pointer turns into a two-headed arrow.

2 Drag the border and drop it when the taskbar is the size you want.

Hide or Display the Taskbar

1 Right-click in an empty part of the taskbar, and choose Properties from the shortcut menu.

2 Turn on the Auto Hide option.

3 Turn on any other options you want.

4 Click OK.

5 Move the mouse pointer to the screen edge where the taskbar is hidden. The taskbar slides into view.

6 Click the buttons you want.

7 Move the mouse pointer off the taskbar to hide the taskbar again.

Displays taskbar on top of other windows.

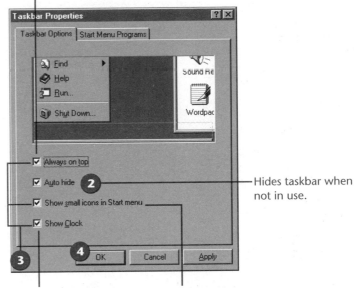

Hides taskbar when not in use.

Displays time on taskbar.

Shows small icons on Start menu instead of large ones.

Placing Documents on the Desktop

The first time you saw your Windows Desktop, it was already equipped with some icons that started programs or that led you quickly to special locations. If there are documents that you use on a regular basis, you can put them on your Desktop to speed up your work.

Move or Copy a Document onto the Desktop

1 Double-click My Computer.

2 Navigate through the folders to find the document you want.

3 Move or copy the document onto the Desktop:

♦ To move, hold down the Shift key, drag the document, drop it on the Desktop, and release the Shift key.

♦ To copy, hold down the Ctrl key, drag the document, drop it on the Desktop, and release the Ctrl key.

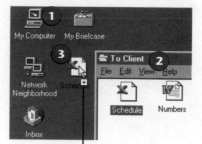

Plus sign shows that the file is being copied.

Save a Document to the Desktop

1. Create the document in your program.

2. Choose Save from the File menu to display the Save As dialog box.

3. Select Desktop from the Save In drop-down list.

4. Type a name for the document.

5. Click the Save button.

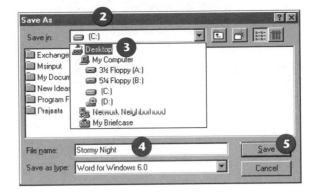

Save Part of a Document to the Desktop

1. Select the part of the document to be saved.

2. Drag the selection and drop it on the Desktop. (You'll notice that Windows puts a "scrap" icon on the Desktop.)

Drag content from here...

...and drop it here.

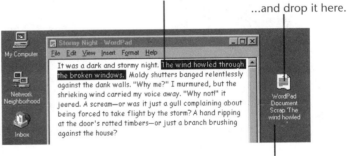

Content stored in scrap can be inserted into a document at a later time.

Placing Shortcuts on the Desktop

You can put shortcuts on your Desktop that give you quick access to almost anything on your computer, to a network, or to items on a company intranet or the Internet. When you create a shortcut, the file or folder stays in its original location—what you put on the Desktop are simply the *directions* on how to find the item. With the shortcut on the Desktop, you have immediate access to the item without having to remember where to find it. You can even customize how the item works when it is accessed.

Create a Shortcut

1 Double-click My Computer or, for a network location, Network Neighborhood.

2 Navigate to find the folder, document, program, or other item for which you want to create the shortcut.

3 Hold down the *right* mouse button, drag the item, and drop it on the Desktop.

4 Choose Create Shortcut(s) Here from the shortcut menu.

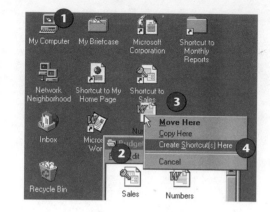

Customize a Shortcut

1 Right-click the shortcut on the Desktop, and choose Properties from the shortcut menu.

2 Change the settings.

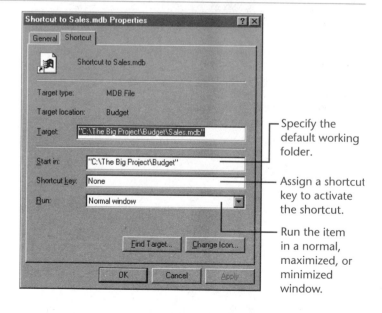

Specify the default working folder.

Assign a shortcut key to activate the shortcut.

Run the item in a normal, maximized, or minimized window.

Change a Shortcut's Appearance

1. Click the Change Icon button to display the Change Icon dialog box.

2. Select a different icon.

3. Click OK.

4. Click OK in the Properties dialog box.

5. Click the shortcut to select it.

6. Click the name of the shortcut, edit the name, and press Enter.

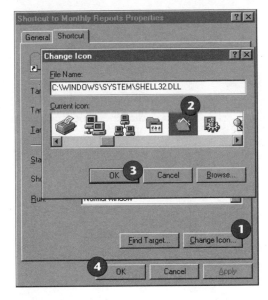

Changing the Look of Icons

There are icons all over the place in Windows, and if you don't care for the way they look, give them a makeover! You can change their size, the distance between them, and even the font and font size of their captions. Any changes that you make apply to all the Windows icons—on your Desktop, in My Computer, and in Windows Explorer.

SEE ALSO

"Exploring Windows" on page 22 and "Sorting the File Listings" on page 24 for information about arranging icons.

TIP

Windows has two preset schemes—Windows Standard (Large) and Windows Standard (Extra Large)—that change the font size but not the icon size or spacing.

Change the Size, Font, and Font Size of Icons

1. Right-click in a blank part of the Desktop, and choose Properties from the shortcut menu.

2. Click the Appearance tab.

3. Select Icon from the Item list.

4. Select a new point size for your icons.

5. Select a different font.

6. Select a different font size.

Standard icon

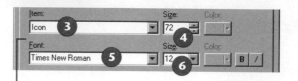

Change the settings.

Custom icon

Increase the Spacing Between Icons

1 Select Icon Spacing (Horizontal) from the Item list.

2 Set a new size.

3 Select Icon Spacing (Vertical) from the Item list.

4 Set a new size.

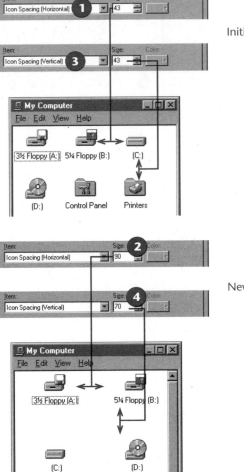

Initial icon spacing

New icon spacing

Changing the Look of the Desktop

Just as your physical desktop might be constructed from solid oak, printed plastic, or glass, your Windows Desktop can have a patterned surface. You can add a picture for even more interest, and have it occupy the entire Desktop surface or only part of it. You can even combine a picture with a patterned background. Keep experimenting until you find the look you like—it's a lot of fun!

Add a Pattern

1 Right-click in a blank part of the Desktop and choose Properties from the shortcut menu.

2 Click the Background tab if it's not already selected.

3 Click (None) in the Wallpaper list.

4 Select the pattern that you want to use from the Pattern list.

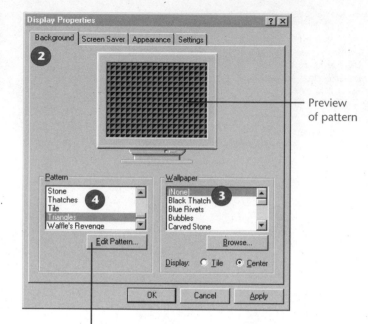

Preview of pattern

Click to customize selected pattern.

SEE ALSO

"Creating Your Own Desktop Wallpaper" on page 72 for information about creating your own wallpaper.

TIP

You can use only bitmap pictures for Desktop patterns and pictures.

TIP

The Wallpaper picture is always on top of the pattern. You'll see the pattern only if the wallpaper picture is centered rather than tiled and the picture is smaller than the whole screen. Alternatively, you can set the wallpaper to (None). If you have the wallpaper and the pattern both set to (None), the Desktop will be a solid color as set on the Appearance tab.

Add a Picture

1. Select the picture you want to use from the Wallpaper list.

2. Click the Display option you want:

   ◆ Tile repeats the image to fill the Desktop.

   ◆ Center places a single copy of the picture in the center of the Desktop.

3. Click OK.

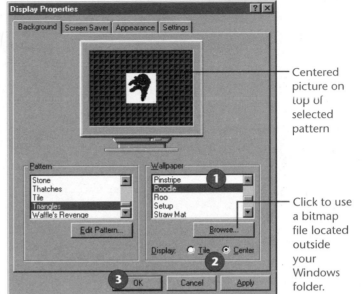

Centered picture on top of selected pattern

Click to use a bitmap file located outside your Windows folder.

Cleaning Up the Desktop

If your Desktop becomes so cluttered with unused shortcuts, old scraps of text, or overlapping icons that you can't find what you want at a glance, take a minute or two to do a little housekeeping.

Delete Folders, Files, Shortcuts, and Scraps

1. Select the item or items to be deleted.

2. Drag the items and drop them on the Recycle Bin icon.

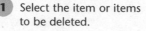

Arrange the Icons

1. Right-click in a blank part of the Desktop.

2. Point to Arrange Icons on the shortcut menu and choose the type of arrangement you want.

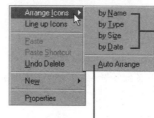

Choose the way you want the icons to be arranged.

Turn on to have Windows automatically arrange icons after you've moved, created, or deleted them.

Create Your Own Arrangement

1. Drag the icons to the area of the Desktop where you want them.

2. Right-click in a blank part of the Desktop.

3. Choose Line Up Icons.

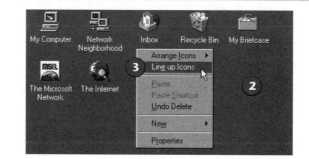

Making More Room on the Desktop

If you want to squeeze more items onto your Desktop, you can change the size of the Desktop...sort of. This is one of those "virtual" realities. You "enlarge" the available space by changing the *scaling,* which lets you fit more items on the Desktop even though its area on your screen doesn't get any larger. Your gain in "virtual" area comes at a cost, though— everything will be smaller and harder to read.

TIP

If Windows has the proper information about your monitor and graphics card, it will display valid settings only. If all the information was not supplied, Windows will try any setting that you create but will cancel the setting if it doesn't work. However, some computers will have only one setting.

Increase the Screen Resolution

1. Right-click in a blank part of the Desktop and choose Properties from the shortcut menu.

2. Click the Settings tab.

3. Drag the Desktop Area slider to the right and drop it at a new setting.

4. Select a font size:
   - ◆ Small Fonts uses the same scaling on fonts that is used on all screen elements.
   - ◆ Large Fonts increases the readability of text.

5. Click OK to apply the changes.

6. Click OK to resize the Desktop.

7. Click Yes to accept the new settings or No to revert to the original settings. If you don't click Yes within 15 seconds, Windows restores the original settings.

8. If you clicked No, click OK to keep the original settings.

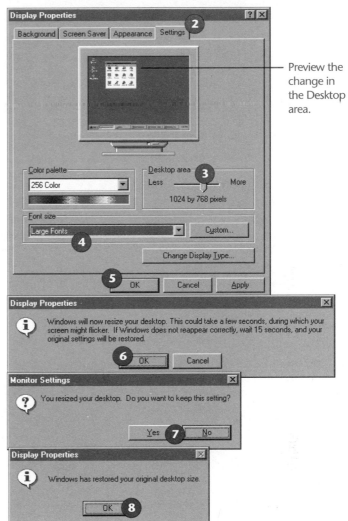

Preview the change in the Desktop area.

Using a Screen Saver

If you work at a computer for hours every day, it's good for your eyes—and for your mental health—to take a break and look at something different once in a while. If you work in an office with other people, you might not want your colleagues to be able to read your screen—albeit unintentionally—any time you're away from your desk for a few minutes. What you need is a screen saver to provide a nice little respite from your work as well as some privacy. If you want to add some security you can use the password option, but then you'll need to enter the password to use the computer when the screen saver is running.

Choose a Screen Saver

1. Right-click in a blank part of the Desktop and choose Properties from the shortcut menu.

2. Click the Screen Saver tab.

3. Select a screen saver.

4. Click Settings to set options for the screen saver.

5. Set the length of time you want your computer to be inactive before the screen saver starts.

6. Click Preview to see the screen saver in full screen.

7. Move your mouse to end the preview.

Preview of screen-saver selection

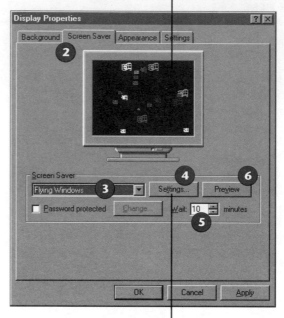

Settings are different for each screen saver.

TIP

Hacked! *The screen-saver password is a useful precaution against prying eyes, but doesn't provide a high level of security. If you want additional security, check your computer's documentation for information about setting up CMOS-based password protection.*

SEE ALSO

"Starting Up" on page 8 for information about starting Windows with a password.

"Changing Your Passwords" on page 190 for information about changing or disabling your password.

TIP

What do you do if you forget your password? Pay the price! Turn off your computer, wait a few seconds, and turn it back on. Return to the Screen Saver tab and change the password to one you'll remember. You'll lose any unsaved work when you turn off the computer, but at least you'll be able to use it again.

Add a Screen-Saver Password

1 Turn on the Password Protected option.

2 Click the Change button.

3 Enter your password twice.

4 Click OK.

5 Click OK.

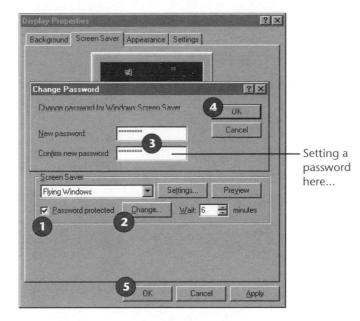

Setting a password here...

...requires entering the same password to remove the screen saver and return to your work.

Changing Screen Colors

If you're tired of looking at the same old colors, you can brighten up—or tone down—the colors on your screen. You can change the Windows color scheme to your own custom-designed color scheme, and you'll see the new colors in your programs.

Define a Color Scheme

1. Right-click in a blank part of the Desktop and choose Properties from the shortcut menu.

2. Click the Appearance tab.

3. Click the items you want to change, or select items from the Item list that weren't displayed in the preview on the Appearance tab.

4. Change the colors.

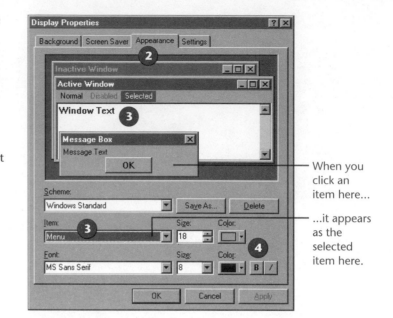

When you click an item here...

...it appears as the selected item here.

Save the Changes

1. Click the Save As button.

2. Type a name for your color scheme.

3. Click OK.

4. Click OK to apply the changes.

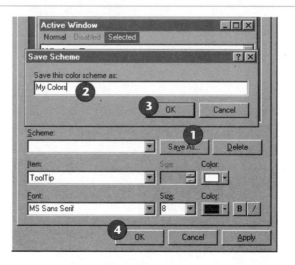

Making Everything More Colorful

Most computers can display different ranges of color, from a simple 16-color palette that's fine for displaying colors in dialog boxes to a more complex 24-bit or 32-bit true-color palette that produces photographic-quality colors. The higher levels of color use up a lot of memory, so—depending on the capabilities of your computer—you might have to work with reduced screen resolution if you need to use the highest color settings.

SEE ALSO

"Making More Room on the Desktop" on page 129 for information about setting the screen resolution.

Change the Color Palette

1. Right-click in a blank part of the Desktop and choose Properties from the shortcut menu.

2. Click the Settings tab.

3. Select a setting in the Color Palette drop-down list.

4. Click OK.

5. Click Yes to restart your computer.

The colors available depend on your computer system.

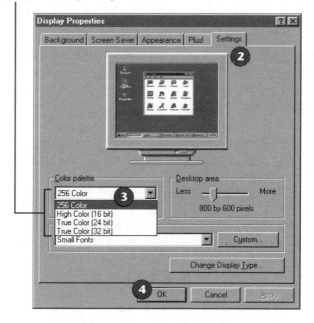

Making the Mouse Pointer More Visible

If you sometimes have difficulty finding the mouse pointer on your screen, you can make the pointer large or even extra large. To help follow the mouse pointer's path, you can also show mouse "trails"—images of the mouse pointer that linger on the screen for a moment after the mouse pointer has been moved.

SEE ALSO

"Customizing Mouse Operations" on page 138 for information about adjusting the mouse configuration.

Change the Mouse Pointer Size

1 Click the Start button, point to Settings, and choose Control Panel from the submenu.

2 Double-click the Mouse icon.

3 Click the Pointers tab.

4 Select a new size from the Scheme drop-down list:

◆ Windows Standard (Extra Large)

◆ Windows Standard (Large)

Mouse Properties

Buttons | Pointers | Motion | General

Scheme **3**

Windows Standard

(None)
3D Pointers
Animated Hourglasses
Entertainment
Food
Mouse
Nature
Ocean
Reptiles
Sports
Windows Standard
Windows Standard (extra large) **4**
Windows Standard (large)

Precision Select

Text Select

Use Default | Browse...

OK | Cancel | Apply

Add Mouse Trails

1 Click the Motion tab.

2 Turn on the Show Pointer Trails option.

3 Drag the slider and drop it to set the length of the trails.

4 Click OK to close the Mouse Properties dialog box.

Mouse Properties

Buttons | Pointers | Motion | General

Pointer speed **1**

Slow ———————— Fast

Pointer trail **2**

☑ Show pointer trails **3**

Short ———————— Long

Changing the Pointer Scheme

Would you like something more exciting than an arrow as a mouse pointer? You can make your work much more entertaining by using different pointers for standard Windows events. Your choices are varied, from three-dimensional pointers to a frankly anthropomorphic and quite adorable animated mouse of the four-legged-and-furry variety.

SEE ALSO

"Creating a Pointer Scheme" on page 136 for information about customizing a pointer scheme.

Change the Pointer Scheme

1 Click the Start button, point to Settings, and choose Control Panel from the submenu.

2 Double-click the Mouse icon.

3 Click the Pointers tab.

4 Select a new scheme from the Scheme drop-down list.

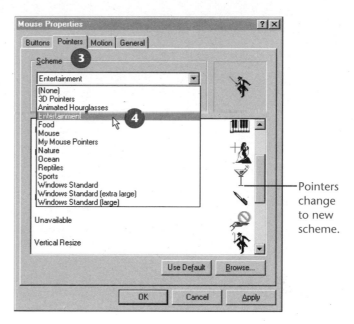

Pointers change to new scheme.

Creating a Pointer Scheme

You can customize your mouse-pointer scheme by replacing one or more of the existing pointers in a scheme with the pointers of your choice. In the example at the right, we changed the "Busy" pointer from piano keys to a coffee cup.

TIP

Windows comes with several additional mouse pointers. If these pointers were not included in your original installation, you can install them at any time.

SEE ALSO

"Changing the Pointer Scheme" on page 135 for information about changing the entire pointer scheme.

Change Individual Pointers

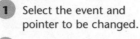 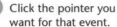

1 Select the event and pointer to be changed.

2 Click Browse.

3 Click the pointer you want for that event.

4 Click Open.

5 Repeat steps 1 through 4 to change other individual pointers.

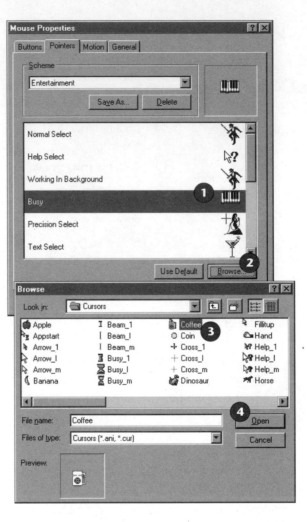

SEE ALSO

"Making the Mouse Pointer More Visible" on page 134 for information about speeding up the pointer and adding pointer trails.

"Adding or Removing Windows Components" on page 156 for information about installing additional Windows components.

TIP

The available mouse-pointer schemes depend on the software that you have installed. Windows 95 comes with five schemes, and Microsoft Intelli-Point mouse software provides additional schemes. Microsoft Plus! for Windows 95 also comes with numerous mouse-pointer schemes.

SEE ALSO

"Switching Desktop Themes" on page 263 and "Creating a Desktop Theme" on page 264 for information about customizing mouse-pointer schemes in the Desktop Themes that come with Microsoft Plus! for Windows 95.

Save Your Scheme

1 Click the Save As button.

2 Type a name for your scheme.

3 Click OK.

4 Click OK to apply the new scheme.

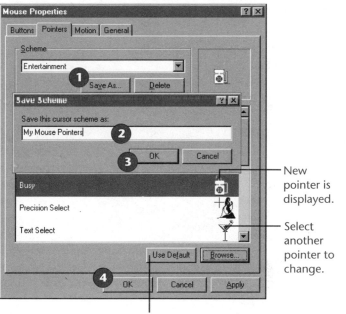

New pointer is displayed.

Select another pointer to change.

Click to restore pointers originally designed for this scheme.

Customizing Mouse Operations

If you spend a lot of time mousing around in your programs, you can make a few minor adjustments that will substantially improve your effectiveness *and* your comfort. You can adjust the configuration of the mouse buttons for left-handed operation, as well as adjusting pointer speed and double-click speed.

Switch Mouse Buttons

1 Click the Start button, point to Settings, and choose Control Panel from the submenu.

2 Double-click the Mouse icon.

3 Click the Buttons tab.

4 Click the appropriate option.

Select the way you use the mouse.

Shows right-button functions based on button configuration.

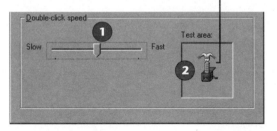

Shows left-button functions based on button configuration.

Set the Double-Click Speed

1 Drag the slider and drop it to set the speed of the double-click.

2 Double-click the jack-in-the-box.

Pops up when double-clicked. If it doesn't pop up, reset the speed and try again.

Set the Pointer Speed

1 Click the Motion tab.

2 Drag the slider and drop it to set the pointer speed.

3 Click OK.

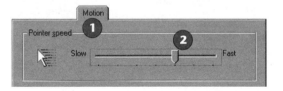

Adjusting the Date and Time

If you take a laptop computer with you when you travel long distances, or if the computer's battery has run down, you'll need to adjust your computer's clock to the correct time zone. If you've had your computer repaired, you'll probably need to correct the date and time.

TIP

If the time isn't shown on the taskbar, double-click the Date/Time icon in the Control Panel to set the date, time, and time zone.

To see whether the date is correct, point to the time on the taskbar and hold the mouse steady until the date appears.

Adjust the Time Zone

1. Double-click the time on the taskbar.

2. Click the Time Zone tab.

3. Click your location on the map.

4. Verify that you selected the correct time zone.

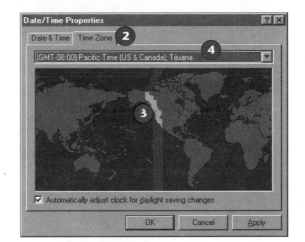

Adjust the Date and Time

1. Click the Date & Time tab.

2. Select the current month from the drop-down list.

3. Select the current year from the drop-down list.

4. Click today's date.

5. Click the hour, minute, second, and AM or PM to be adjusted.

6. Use the arrows to adjust the time.

7. Verify the time on the clock face.

8. Click OK.

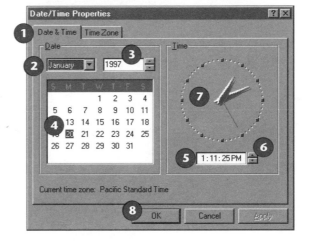

8

Adjusting Settings for a Different Region

If you are working in, or producing documents for use in, a region or country other than the one for which your computer was originally configured, you can change the default region and have Windows automatically adjust the numbering, currency, time, and date schemes used by your programs.

TIP

You must restart the computer after changing the default region before you can customize the settings.

Change the Default Region

1. Click the Start button, point to Settings, and choose Control Panel from the submenu.

2. Double-click the Regional Settings icon to display the Regional Settings Properties dialog box.

3. On the Regional Settings tab, select the language and, if necessary, the associated country.

4. Click OK.

5. Click Yes to restart the computer.

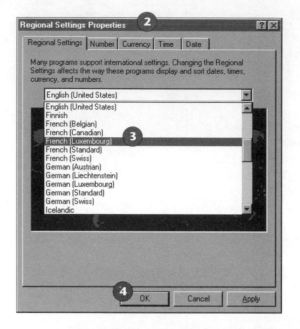

Customize the Settings

1 Open the Control Panel if it's not already open, and double-click the Regional Settings icon.

2 Use the Number, Currency, Time, and Date tabs to customize the regional settings.

3 Click Apply after each change.

4 Click OK when you've finished.

Changing the Date and Time Format

Windows uses the most commonly accepted ways to display date and time, but you can change the display to the format you prefer.

```
DATE FORMATS
2/5/97
or
02/05/1997
or
Feb 5, 1997

TIME FORMATS
3:05:30 P
or
03:05:30 PM
or
15:05:30
```

SEE ALSO

"Adjusting Settings for a Different Region" on page 140 for information about changing settings for a different region or country and language.

Change the Date Format

1. Click the Start button, point to Settings, and choose Control Panel from the submenu.

2. Double-click the Regional Settings icon.

3. Click the Date tab.

4. Select or type a different format for the short date. See the table at the right for valid codes.

5. Click Apply.

6. Select or type a different separator for the short date.

7. Click Apply.

8. Select or type a different format for the long date.

9. Click Apply.

CODES FOR DATE FORMATS	
Code	**Result**
M	Month number
MM	Month number, always two digits
MMM	Three-letter month abbreviation
MMMM	Full month name
d	Day number
dd	Day number, always two digits
ddd	Three-letter day abbreviation
dddd	Full day name
yy	Year number, last two digits only
yyyy	Full year number

TRY THIS

Select or create date and time formats, and apply them. Then switch to a folder window, display file information by using the Details view, and look at the modified date and time. Change the date and time formats, and note the difference in the folder window.

Change the Time Format

1 Click the Time tab.

2 Select or type a different format for the time. See the table at the right for valid codes.

3 Click Apply.

4 Select or type a different separator for the time.

5 Click Apply.

6 Select or type a different AM symbol.

7 Click Apply.

8 Select or type a different PM symbol.

9 Click Apply.

CODES FOR TIME FORMATS	
Code	**Result**
h	Hour in 12-hour format
hh	Hour in 12-hour format, always two digits
ll	Hour in 24-hour format
HH	Hour in 24-hour format, always two digits
m	Minute
mm	Minute, always two digits
s	Second
ss	Second, always two digits
t	AM or PM symbol, first character only
tt	AM or PM symbol, all characters

Using a Different-Language Keyboard

If you are working in, or producing documents for use in, a country other than the one for which your computer was originally configured, you can install a keyboard configured for that country's language. After you've installed the keyboard, you simply indicate which keyboard you're using, and Windows will use the correct characters for that keyboard.

TIP

You can use your normal keyboard with any language setting. If you're using a keyboard that doesn't match the language setting, you need to remember which keys produce the characters you want.

Add a Keyboard Layout

1. Click the Start button, point to Settings, and choose Control Panel from the submenu.

2. Double-click the Keyboard icon to display the Keyboard Properties dialog box.

3. Click the Language tab.

4. Click the Add button.

5. Select the language and, if necessary, the country.

6. Click OK.

7. Turn on the Enable Indicator On Taskbar check box.

8. Click OK.

9. Insert the requested Windows disk or CD into the correct drive, and click OK.

Switch Layouts

1. Click the keyboard layout abbreviation on the taskbar.

2. Select the keyboard layout you want.

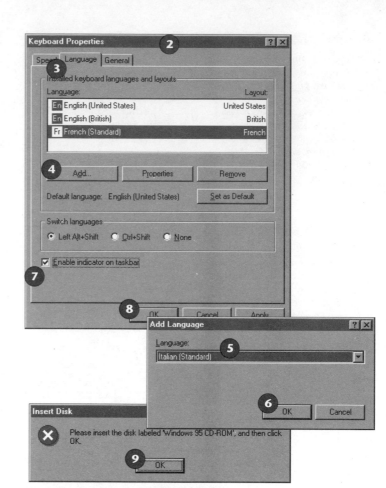

Saving Disk Space by Frequent Recycling

When you delete files from your hard disk, they are stored in the Recycle Bin until you empty the bin, or until the bin becomes full and the oldest files are automatically deleted. If you don't need to keep deleted files for a long time, you can save disk space by reducing the maximum size of the Recycle Bin.

TIP

To see if your Recycle Bin is too large, open it and, in Details view, see if the bin contains a lot of old files that you'll never need. If so, you could use a smaller Recycle Bin.

Change the Recycle Bin Size

1 Right-click the Recycle Bin icon on your Desktop and choose Properties from the shortcut menu.

2 Drag the slider to the left and drop it to set a smaller size.

3 Click OK.

Click this option and use tabs to change the setting for each drive independently.

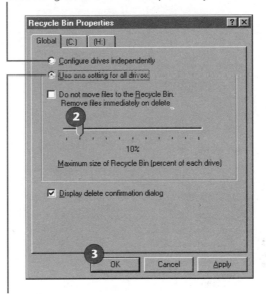

Click this option and adjust here to change settings for all drives.

Specifying Which Program Opens a Document

When you double-click a document, it usually opens in its associated program—a Microsoft Word document opens in Word, a bitmap image opens in Paint, and so on. Sometimes, however, you might want one type of document to open in a different program—perhaps you want text documents to open in WordPad instead of in Notepad, for example. You can make this happen by associating the file type with a program.

> **TIP**
>
> *The types of files listed on the File Types tab depend on the programs you have installed.*

Select the File Type

1 Double-click My Computer.

2 Choose Options from the View menu to display the Options dialog box.

3 Click the File Types tab.

4 Select the file type whose association you want to change.

5 Click the Edit button.

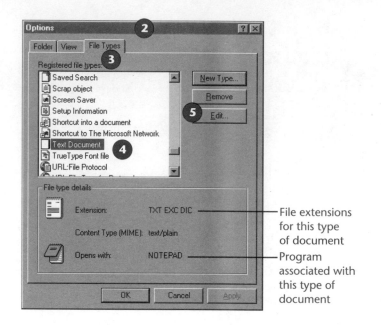

File extensions for this type of document

Program associated with this type of document

When you double-click a file that has no registered association, the Open With dialog box appears. Use it to stipulate which program the file will be used with.

Edit the Association

1 Select Open in the Actions list.

2 Click the Edit button.

3 Click the Browse button.

4 Navigate through your folders and select the program in which you want your document to open.

5 Click Open to specify the program.

6 Click OK to set the association.

7 Click Close to end the editing.

8 Click Close to close the Options dialog box.

Click to use a different icon for this file type.

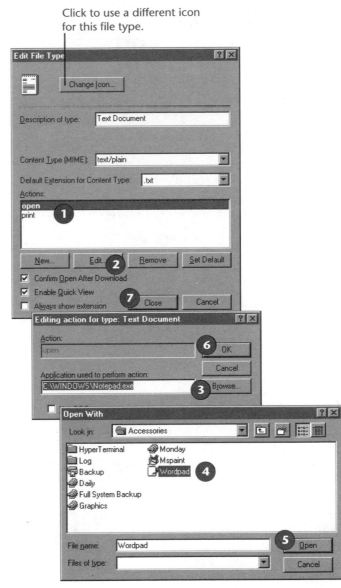

File Associations, File Extensions, and Registered Programs

Windows tries hard to let your work be *docu-centric*—that is, you concentrate on keeping your *documents* organized and Windows will do the work of figuring out which *programs* your documents need to run. To do this, Windows needs three main pieces of information:

◆ The programs you have installed

◆ The types of documents that are to be opened in each program

◆ The file type of the document you want to use

Windows keeps track of all this information in a special database called the *registry*. Whenever you run Setup to install a software program, Setup adds information to the registry, including the name and location of the program and the types of documents and files the program will open.

To link a document with a program, Windows uses the file's extension—the three-character code that follows the document's name—to identify the document as a specific file type. The file's extension, which is usually added automatically when you save a document in a program, might or might not be visible, depending on your settings, but Windows is always aware of it. (See "Displaying MS-DOS Information" on page 43 and "Hiding System Files" on page 44 for information about displaying a file's extension.) By recognizing the file extension, Windows knows the file type of the document and its associated program.

You can identify the file type of a document by its icon and, when you're in Details view, by the description in the Type column. Because a document is identified by its extension, you shouldn't change the extension when you create a document or when you are conducting any file management. Sometimes, alas, things don't work out as they're supposed to. Some programs are installed without the use of Setup and thus might not be registered. Other programs can grab a file extension that "belongs to" another program. And sometimes, even when Setup is used, a program somehow doesn't register itself correctly.

When a program isn't properly registered, whatever the reason, you can often solve the problem by rerunning Setup for the program or by changing the file extension's program association, as described in "Specifying Which Program Opens a Document" on page 146. If neither of these methods works, contact the software vendors. They might be able to supply you with updated software that properly registers the program, or they might tell you how to fix the problem with a workaround. But remember—it's *very* dangerous to edit the settings in the registry. If anyone suggests that you do this, the first thing you should do when you run RegEdit is to make a copy of the registry, using the Export Registry File command on the File menu. That way, if something goes wrong, you can restore the original registry.

EXAMPLES OF FILES AND THEIR EXTENSIONS

Document type	Icon	Filename with extension
Text document	Status	Status.txt
Bitmap image	Plans	Plans.bmp
Wave sound	My Message	My Message.wav
MS-DOS program	MyProg	MyProg.exe
Internet document (HTML)	My Home Page	My Home Page.htm

Remodeling Your System

As time goes on, you'll probably want—or need—to do some remodeling of your system. You might want to add or delete some Windows 95 components. Perhaps you want to upgrade to a new version of a favorite program, add new programs or hardware, or even restructure what's already there. If you always start your work day using one particular program, you can put that program in the StartUp folder, and it will start automatically when Windows starts. Or you can add items to or remove them from the Start menu. If you're fond of the Documents menu because it's such a speedy way to access the documents you're using in your current project, you can wipe it clean when you start a new project, and you won't have to search through out-of-date documents. You can install the fonts you know and love, and remove the ones whose looks you can't stand.

Just as when you're remodeling a house, however, you need to use the right tools to get the job done quickly and efficiently. Fortunately, Windows comes fully equipped with the tools you need, and often takes over the entire operation for you.

Some of the tools—the Installation Wizard, the Add New Hardware Wizard, and the Add Printer Wizard, for example—simply ask you to respond to a series of questions as they do the job for you.

Starting a Program When Windows Starts

If you always start your work day using the same program, you can have that program start automatically when Windows starts. This means that Windows will take a little longer to load, but your program will be ready for you to start working on right away.

Add a Program to Windows StartUp

1. Right-click in a blank part of the taskbar and choose Properties from the shortcut menu.

2. On the Start Menu Programs tab, click Add.

3. Type the path and program name, or use the Browse button to locate the program. Click Next.

4. Select the StartUp folder, and click Next.

5. Type the name of the program, and click Finish.

6. Click OK.

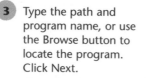

Select a Title for the Program ? X

Select a name for the shortcut:

MS Exchange ⑤

Select Program Folder ? X

Select folder to place shortcut in:

- Accessories
  - Fax
  - Games
  - Internet Tools
  - Multimedia
  - System Tools
- Microsoft Input Devices
  - Mouse
- Office 97
- StartUp ④

Create Shortcut ? X

Type the location and name of the item you want to create a shortcut to. Or, search for the item by clicking Browse.

Command line:

"C:\Program Files\Microsoft Exchange\Exchng32.exe"

Browse... ③

Taskbar Properties ? X

Taskbar Options | Start Menu Programs

Customize Start Menu

You may customize your Start Menu by adding or removing items from it.

② Add... | Remove... | Advanced...

Documents Menu

Click the Clear button to remove the contents of the Documents Menu.

Clear

⑥ OK | Cancel | Apply

Adding an Item to the Start Menu

When you open the Start menu, the item you're looking for is usually on one of the cascading submenus. You can add items to the submenus and you can even create your own submenus. Windows uses folders to organize the Start menu, and each folder contained in the Start Menu folder creates a submenu. So, to access an item from a submenu, you add a shortcut to the item in the appropriate folder.

TIP

To add a document instead of a program to the Start menu, select All Files from the Files Of Type list in the Browse dialog box.

SEE ALSO

"Creating and Working with Shortcuts" on page 40 for information about adding shortcuts to the Start menu.

Add Access from a Submenu

1 Right-click in a blank part of the taskbar and choose Properties from the shortcut menu.

2 On the Start Menu Programs tab, click Add.

3 Click the Browse button to find the program.

4 Select the program, and click the Open button.

5 Verify the program's path and filename, and click Next.

6 Select the folder—and therefore the submenu—that will contain the program, and click Next.

7 Type the program name that you want to appear on the submenu, and click Finish.

8 Click OK in the Taskbar Properties dialog box.

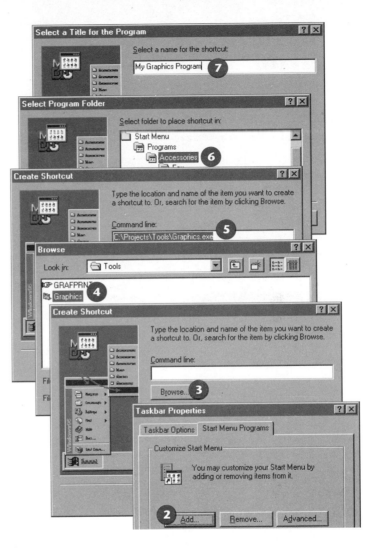

Removing an Item from the Start Menu

If there are shortcuts that you no longer need on the Start menu, or if you don't want to keep the shortcuts that were added during the installation of a program, you can remove them.

TIP

In almost all cases, the Start menu contains shortcuts to programs. Removing an item from the Start menu doesn't remove the program itself— it removes only the shortcut. If you don't want the program any longer, you should un- install it.

SEE ALSO

"Removing a Software Pro- gram" on page 159 for infor- mation about uninstalling programs.

Remove an Item from the Start Menu

1. Right-click in a blank part of the taskbar and choose Properties from the shortcut menu.

2. On the Start Menu Programs tab, click Remove.

3. Open the folder containing the item to be removed.

4. Select the item.

5. Click Remove.

6. Repeat steps 3 through 5 to remove all unwanted items.

7. Click Close.

8. Click OK.

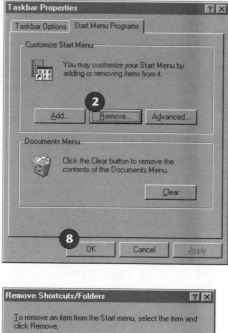

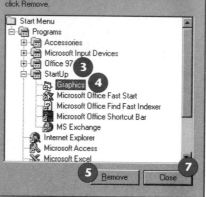

Removing the Contents of the Documents Menu

Using the Documents menu is a quick and handy way to access your most recently used documents. But some-times—when you start a new project, for example—you don't want to sort through a menu of documents that are unrelated to your current project. You can start out with a clean slate by resetting the Documents menu.

Reset the Documents Menu

1 Right-click in a blank part of the taskbar and choose Properties from the shortcut menu.

2 On the Start Menu Programs tab, click the Clear button.

3 Click OK.

4 Click the Start button, point to Documents, and verify that the menu is empty.

Adding or Removing Windows Components

As you work, you might find that some Windows 95 components you'd like to use aren't installed on your computer. Or perhaps there are Windows components installed that you never use. You don't have to run the Windows Setup program again—you can use the tools Windows provides to install or remove any Windows components.

TIP

To install components, you'll need to have your Windows CD or Setup disks available.

Add or Remove a Component Group

1 Save any documents that you're working on, and close all your running programs.

2 Click the Start button, point to Settings, and choose Control Panel from the submenu.

3 Double-click the Add/Remove Programs icon.

4 On the Windows Setup tab, turn check boxes on or off to add or remove all the items in the component group.

Click a checked box to turn off the option and remove all items from the group.

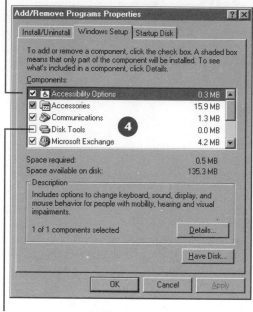

Click an unchecked box to turn on the option and add all items to the group.

Add or Remove an Item in a Component Group

1 Select the component group where you want to add or remove an item.

2 Click Details.

3 Click a checked box to remove the item, or click an unchecked box to add the item.

4 Click OK when you've finished adding or removing the item or items.

5 Repeat steps 1 through 4 for each component group you want to change.

6 Click OK.

Installing a Software Program

Most software programs have an installation program that copies the required files to the hard disk and tells Windows which files are installed, where they are, and what they do. Windows simplifies the installation of most Windows-based programs and many MS-DOS–based programs with the helpful Installation Wizard. Before you start, however, look at the program documentation for installation instructions. It's better to avoid problems in the beginning so that you don't have to fix them later.

Install a Program

1. Save any documents that you're working on, and close all your running programs.

2. Click the Start button, point to Settings, and choose Control Panel from the submenu.

3. Double-click the Add/Remove Programs icon.

4. Click Install.

5. Place the installation disk or the CD in your drive, and click Next.

6. If the correct Setup program filename is displayed, click Finish. If not, click Browse, locate the Setup program, and then click Finish.

7. Follow the Setup program's instructions.

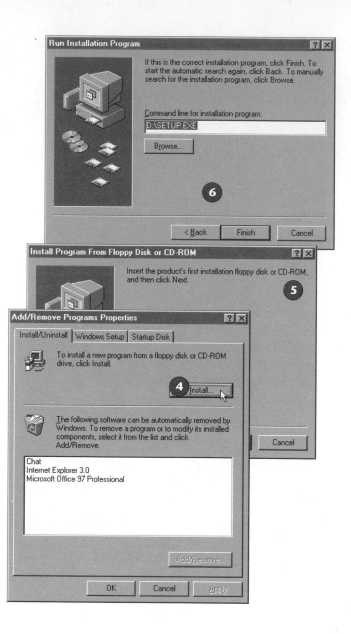

Removing a Software Program

Most software programs are "registered" with Windows when you install them. You can—and should—use Windows tools to remove a program. If you simply delete the files, you might leave accessory files you don't need, or delete files that you need for other programs. When you use Windows tools to *uninstall* a program, Windows keeps track of the files you need. When a file is no longer needed by any of your programs, Windows deletes the file.

SEE ALSO

"File Associations, File Extensions, and Registered Programs" on pages 148–149 for information about registered programs.

"Adding or Removing Windows Components" on page 156 for information about removing Windows components.

Uninstall a Program

1 Save any documents that you're working on, and close all your running programs.

2 Click the Start button, point to Settings, and choose Control Panel from the submenu.

3 Double-click the Add/Remove Programs icon.

4 On the Install/Uninstall tab, select the program to be uninstalled. (Programs that are components of Windows itself—Paint and WordPad, for example— aren't listed here. You can remove them using the Windows Setup tab.)

5 Click Add/Remove. (If the program you want to remove isn't listed on the Install/Uninstall tab, see the program's documentation for removal instructions.)

6 Follow the instructions that appear on the screen.

7 Click OK when you've finished.

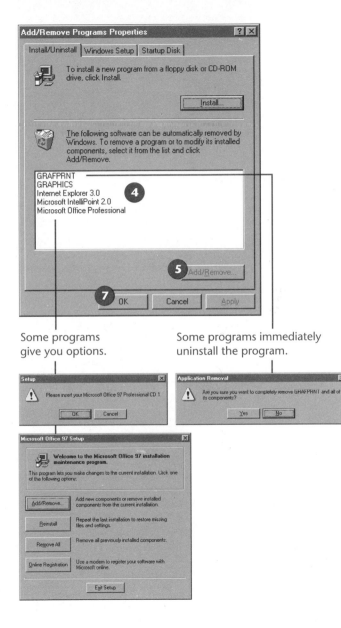

Some programs give you options.

Some programs immediately uninstall the program.

Adding Fonts to Your System

Fonts are styles of lettering whose different designs add personality and feeling to our words. Some programs offer many fonts on a CD that you can install as you need them. Windows makes it easy to install fonts and to view them on screen. You can print very nice sample sheets and store them in a binder—a handy reference tool when you're trying to decide which fonts to use.

Add a Font

1. Click the Start button, point to Settings, choose Control Panel, and double-click the shortcut to the Fonts folder.

2. Choose Install New Font from the File menu.

3. Navigate to the drive and folder containing the font to be installed.

4. Select the font or fonts.

5. Click OK.

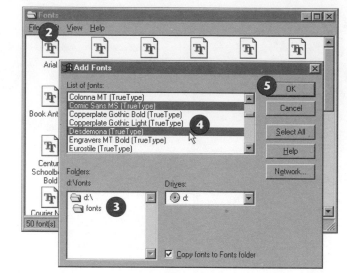

View and Print a Font

1. Double-click the font name to view a font sample.

2. Click Print to print a font sample sheet.

3. Click Done.

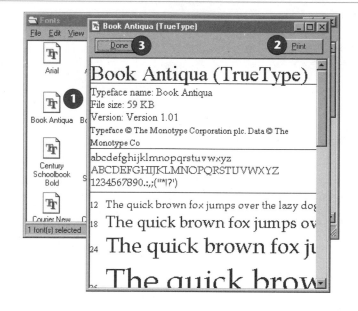

Adding a Printer to Your Computer

If you're adding a new printer to your computer, you need to let Windows know about it. Some printers are Plug and Play (PNP) components and are automatically set up to work with Windows when you restart your computer. For non–Plug and Play printers, you use the Add Printer Wizard to set up the printer.

SEE ALSO

"Adding New Equipment" on page 164 for information about installing a Plug and Play printer.

"Sharing a Printer" on page 178 for information about sharing your printer with people in your workgroup, and "Connecting to a Network Printer" on page 179 for information about connecting to a network printer.

Add a Printer

1 Turn off your computer, install the printer, and turn your computer back on.

2 Click the Start button, point to Settings, and choose Printers from the submenu.

3 Double-click the Add Printer icon, and click Next in the first screen of the Add Printer Wizard.

4 Select Local Printer if the printer is directly connected to your computer. Click Next.

5 Select the manufacturer and the printer model. Click Next.

6 Select the port to which the printer is connected, and click Next.

7 Complete the remaining steps of the wizard, configuring the printer for the way you'll be using it.

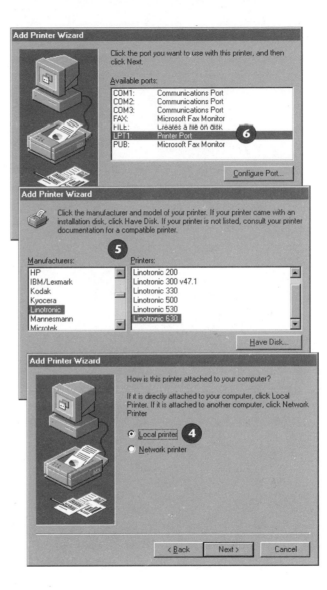

Hooked on Fonts

When you open the Font drop-down list on a program's toolbar, you might be surprised to see how many fonts you already have. Where did they all come from? Well, Windows 95 comes with quite a few fonts, and if you've installed other programs, you've probably installed their font collections too. Depending on where your fonts came from, you'll see various icons—or in some cases no icon at all—next to their names in the Font list. The two icons you'll see most frequently represent TrueType fonts and printer fonts. (Windows also includes a few other fonts that are provided for compatibility with some older programs.)

◆ TrueType fonts are WYSIWYG (what-you-see-is-what-you-get) fonts, which means that the printed output looks exactly the same as what you see on your screen. TrueType fonts are outline fonts: the shapes of the letters are drawn with lines and curves rather than with patterns of dots. TrueType fonts were designed to print well at any size on almost any printer, even at low resolutions.

◆ Printer fonts are stored in your printer, not in your computer's Fonts folder. When you install a printer, these fonts are made available to your programs, and their names appear in your Font list. Be aware, if you're using a printer font, that what you see on your screen might not exactly match your printed output—sometimes you'll see a look-alike font instead.

What these rather dry facts don't tell you is what a delight it is to be able to transform the look and the personality of your text with a few mouse-clicks. Try it! Select some text, open your Font drop-down list, click a font name, and see what you get. Open the Font Size list and click to change the size. For a real surprise, try one of the picture fonts. Your words will change into a series of little pictures (called *dingbats*), and you can enlarge them, italicize them, and so on, just as you can words. It can be a lot of fun.

If you feel like a kid with a new toy, just keep in mind that you *can* have too much of a good thing. A document with too many different fonts can be very difficult to read, and it instantly marks you as an amateur in the world of graphic design. Keep things simple. Professional designers seldom use more than two or three different fonts in a document—a *display font* for headlines or anything that's meant to attract attention, a *text font* for the body of the document, and perhaps a third font for elements such as captions, pull quotes, sidebars, and so on.

There are literally *thousands* of fonts, and new ones are being created all the time. To learn more about fonts and their history, you'll find the shelves of your local library or bookstore overflowing with fascinating books.

A discussion about the best fonts to use for display or text is beyond the scope of this book, but you won't go wrong if you use a big, bold font for display and a plain, readable font for text.

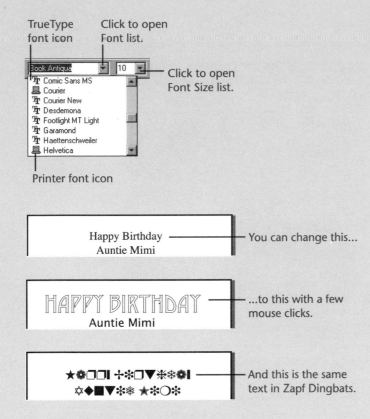

TrueType font icon

Click to open Font list.

Book Antiqua ▼ | 10 ▼

Click to open Font Size list.

𝐓𝐓 Comic Sans MS
▤ Courier
𝐓𝐓 Courier New
𝐓𝐓 Desdemona
𝐓𝐓 Footlight MT Light
𝐓𝐓 Garamond
𝐓𝐓 Haettenschweiler
▤ Helvetica

Printer font icon

Happy Birthday
Auntie Mimi

— You can change this...

HAPPY BIRTHDAY
Auntie Mimi

— ...to this with a few mouse clicks.

★❀▢▢❙ ✛✳▢▼✳✸❀❙
✿◆■▼✳✳ ★✳○✳

— And this is the same text in Zapf Dingbats.

Stormy Night

It was a dark and stormy night. The wind howled through the broken windows. Moldy shutters banged relentlessly against the dank walls. "Why me?" I murmured, but the shrieking wind carried my voice away. "Why not!" it jeered. A scream—or was it just a gull complaining about being forced to take flight by the storm? A hand ripping at the door's rotted timbers—or just a branch brushing against the house?

Stormy Night

It was a dark and stormy night. The wind howled through the broken windows. Moldy shutters banged relentlessly against the dank walls. "Why me?" I murmured, but the shrieking wind carried my voice away. "Why not!" it jeered. A scream—or was it just a gull complaining about being forced to take flight by the storm? A hand ripping at the door's rotted timbers—or just a branch brushing against the house?

Stormy Night

It was a dark and stormy night. The wind howled through the broken windows. Moldy shutters banged relentlessly against the dank walls. "Why me?" I murmured, but the shrieking wind carried my voice away. "Why not!" it jeered. A scream—or was it just a gull complaining about being forced to take flight by the storm? A hand ripping at the door's rotted timbers—or just a branch brushing against the house?

Three different looks created with display and text fonts

9

Adding New Equipment

When you upgrade your computer by adding new equipment, you must inform Windows about the change so that Windows can work with the new hardware. This has become a very simple operation with Plug and Play (PNP) hardware components because all the configuration settings are done automatically. You can, however, install equipment of the non–Plug and Play variety using the Add New Hardware Wizard.

> **TIP**
>
> *The Add New Hardware Wizard might ask you to insert your Windows 95 disks during the installation of new hardware.*

> **TIP**
>
> *If the Add New Hardware Wizard doesn't detect your hardware, see the documentation that came with the hardware, or contact the hardware vendor.*

Plug and Play!

With your computer turned off, install the equipment according to its instructions, and then turn the computer back on.

Add Other Kinds of Equipment

1 Turn off your computer, install the equipment, and turn your computer back on.

2 Click the Start button, point to Settings, and choose Control Panel from the submenu.

3 Double-click the Add New Hardware icon, and click Next in the first screen of the Add New Hardware Wizard.

4 Click Yes to let Windows search for the hardware. Click Next, and continue through the steps of the wizard.

5 After Windows has detected your hardware, click the Details button.

6 Click Next.

7 Click Finish.

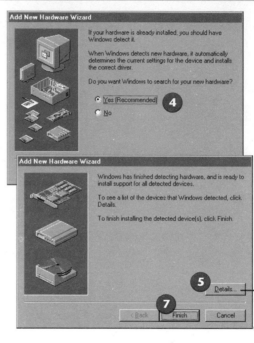

If the information Windows has detected is incorrect, click the Change button, select the correct hardware, and click OK.

10

Networking

No, this isn't about the kind of networking that involves schmoozing with people at power breakfasts or "working the tables" at luncheons, handing out business cards and trying to get the inside track on everything. This is a lot better!

From your computer network, you can reach out and communicate with people in your immediate workgroup or, if you work for a company that has national or international branches, with people in distant parts of the country or on the other side of the world.

You're all part of the Windows 95 Network Neighborhood—and that makes it possible for you to exchange information quickly and productively with your co-workers in Athens, Georgia or Athens, Greece. You can even "chat" on line with people across the network. Although the type of network you're connected to affects exactly what you can do, the way in which you do everything is fairly standardized.

This section of the book will guide you through most of what you'll want or need to do if you're new to networking. If you need help setting up your computer to work on a network, or if you're already set up but are experiencing problems, read your company's networking guidelines or talk to your network administrator.

Different Ways of Networking

Working with networks means that you could be dealing with a *client-server* network system, a *peer-to-peer* network system, or both. What's the difference?

A client-server network is the conventional corporate-type network in which a computer (the server) *hosts,* or provides network services to, other computers (the clients). Almost everything on the network has to pass through the server, which is at the center of this networking universe. The server is managed by a tyrannical overlord known as the *network administrator,* who dictates what each client is allowed to do on the network and can sometimes even prescribe how each client computer is set up.

Servers in a client-server network are often linked so that users have access to other servers. A collection of servers is usually grouped into a management unit called a *domain.* When you log on, you are usually logging on to a domain, which gives you access to all the servers and computers that are part of that domain. Because so many different programs are used to run networks, and because the network administrator can customize the system, you need to refer to your company's network guides for the technical details about using your network.

A peer-to-peer network, as its name implies, is a more democratic network structure. In this kind of network, all computers are created equal and the users of the computers decide whether and what they will share with others. Any computer in the group can be a server (sharing its printer or its files, for example), a client (using someone else's fax modem), or both. When you connect to another computer in a workgroup, either as part of a larger network or as a small stand-alone network, you are using peer-to-peer networking.

Why the different systems? It's mostly a matter of scale. Peer-to-peer systems are the easiest to use but can quickly become overloaded as computers are added to the workgroup. A client-server system with one or more powerful server computers and sophisticated management software is designed to handle very large volumes of network traffic.

A generally accepted standard is that for a small office with 10 or fewer computers, you'll probably want a stand-alone peer-to-peer network. For a company with more than 10 computers, you'll probably need a client-server network set up with workgroups.

Client-Server Network

Peer-to-Peer Network

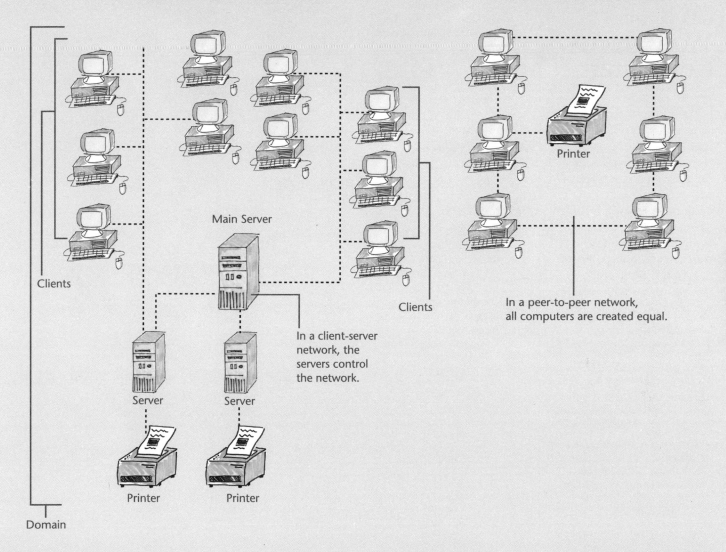

Clients

Main Server

In a client-server network, the servers control the network.

Clients

Server

Server

Printer

Printer

Domain

Printer

In a peer-to-peer network, all computers are created equal.

10

Accessing a Document on a Workgroup Computer

Just as My Computer is the gateway to everything that resides on your computer, Network Neighborhood is the gateway to everything you need on your network. Because what you probably need most often are documents from members of your workgroup, the easiest neighborhood to reach via the network is your own workgroup.

SEE ALSO

"Locating a File by Name" on page 30 and "Locating a File by Date or Content" on page 32 for information about finding files and folders.

"Setting Up a Computer for Different Users" on page 116 for information about what a network administrator can do to your computer and what you can do about it.

Access a Computer

1. Double-click the Network Neighborhood icon on your Windows Desktop to display the Network Neighborhood window.

2. Double-click the computer you want to access.

Access a Folder

1. Navigate to find the folder, if necessary.

2. Double-click the folder.

3. If requested, supply the password to access the folder, and click OK. (Note that you can't access folders on other computers unless the folders have been set up to be shared.)

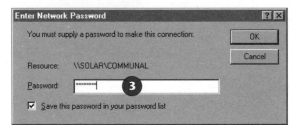

Accessing a Document on a Network Computer

The Windows 95 Network Neighborhood gives you access to more than just your workgroup. By venturing out and exploring the network, you can connect to any computer that is set up to be accessed from the network.

SEE ALSO

"Finding a Computer" on page 170 for information about finding and connecting to a specific computer.

Access a Computer

1. Double-click the Network Neighborhood icon on your Windows Desktop.

2. If the computer isn't listed, double-click Entire Network to display the Entire Network window.

3. If the computer isn't listed, double-click the workgroup that contains the computer.

4. Double-click the computer you want to access.

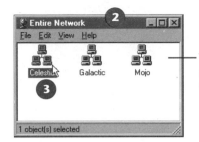

The Entire Network window shows all the workgroups on the network.

Access a Folder

1. Navigate to find the folder, if necessary.

2. Double-click the folder.

3. If asked, supply the password to access the folder, and click OK.

Window for the Mainserver computer in the Celestial workgroup

10

Finding a Computer

If you know the name of a computer that you want to connect to, but it's not part of your workgroup, you can search for that computer by name instead of wandering around the network hoping to stumble across it.

TIP

Because of the way some networks are set up, you might not be able to find a computer that is connected to the network. In such a situation, you might be able to find the computer by typing its full address, in the form \\workgroup\computer or \\computer\share (substituting the actual names of the workgroup, computer, or share, depending on the network setup), in the Named box.

Search for a Computer

1. Click the Start button, point to Find, and choose Computer from the submenu.

2. Type the name of the computer.

3. Click Find Now.

4. Double-click the found computer to access it.

Searching for a computer by its name...

...locates the computer...   ...and shows you its workgroup location.

Creating Quick Access to a Network Resource

If you frequently need access to another computer, or to a folder that's on another computer, you can either create a shortcut to the folder or assign a drive letter to the folder. Although the shortcut is the easiest connection, you might want to assign a drive letter when you're using certain programs. How do you know which way to go? When you want direct access to a folder, create a shortcut. When you're working with a program that requires a drive letter to access network resources, assign a drive letter.

Create a Shortcut

1. Double-click the Network Neighborhood icon on your Windows Desktop.

2. Locate the computer and the folder you want.

3. Click the folder to select it.

4. Hold down the right mouse button, drag the folder, and drop it on the Desktop.

5. Choose Create Shortcut(s) Here from the shortcut menu.

Assign a Drive Letter

1. Click the folder to select it.

2. Choose Map Network Drive from the File menu.

3. Click OK.

Dropping the folder on your Desktop and creating a shortcut...

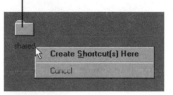

...creates easy access to a folder on another computer.

Select a different unused drive letter if you want.

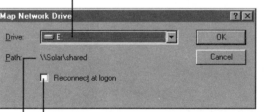

Turn on if you want to create this connection each time you log on to the network.

Check the path to verify that you've connected to the correct computer and folder.

10

Opening Your Computer to Other Users

If you need to share files that are on your computer, or if you want to let co-workers use your printer, you must set up your network connection to allow access by others to your computer. There are two ways to do this: you can create password-only access to certain folders, or you can specify the names of those individuals on your network who are allowed to access the folders.

TIP

You can have only one type of access control for your computer, so make your choice before you start sharing folders. If you change your mind and switch the type of access control, all the folders that were shared will no longer be shared.

Turn On Sharing

1 Click the Start button, point to Settings, and choose Control Panel from the submenu.

2 Double-click the Network icon to display the Network dialog box.

3 On the Configuration tab, select your network.

4 Click the File And Print Sharing button.

5 Specify the items you want to be able to share.

6 Click OK.

7 Click OK.

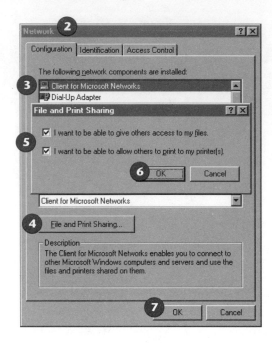

Select the Type of Sharing

1 In the Network dialog box, click the Access Control tab.

2 Select the type of sharing you want:

◆ Share Level, to specify the level of access for each folder.

◆ User Level, to specify which users can access each folder. This requires connection to a server that verifies user names and permissions.

3 Click OK.

4 Restart your computer to implement the changes.

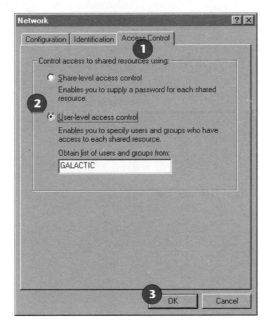

10

Sharing Folders Using Passwords

When you set up your computer for *share-level access control*, you specify which folders are to be shared and what type of access you will allow. You create a password to limit access to the specified folders, and give the password to the people who may access those folders. You can customize the level of access even further by creating one password for full access and another password for read-only access.

SEE ALSO

"Opening Your Computer to Other Users" on page 172 for information about setting up your computer to share folders.

"Sharing Folders with Individuals" on page 176 for information about specifying individual access to shared folders.

Share a Folder

1. Locate the folder you want to share.

2. Right-click the folder, and choose Sharing from the shortcut menu.

3. On the Sharing tab, click the Shared As option.

4. Type a name for the folder.

5. Type a comment if you want one.

6. Select the type of access.

7. Enter the password or passwords required for access:

   ◆ A Read-Only Password if you selected the Read-Only or Depends On Password option

   ◆ A Full Access Password if you selected the Full or Depends On Password option

8. Click OK.

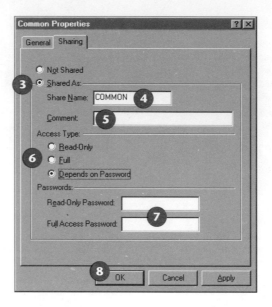

If you forget the password, you can change it from your computer by returning to the Sharing dialog box. But this time, write it down!

You can prevent unauthorized changes to your shared files but still make them available for viewing without a password. For the access type, select Depends On Password. Then specify a Full Access password, but leave Read-Only Password blank. Users who enter the correct password will be granted full access; those who cancel the password prompt can open, but not change the content of, shared files.

Turning on a file's Read-Only option will prevent a user from accidentally saving changes, but be aware that a user can still make changes intentionally by turning off the Read-Only option. When it's critical to protect a file from changes, place it in a folder that is shared with Read-Only access. Then you alone can change the contents of the file.

Protect Individual Files

1 Select the files you want to protect.

2 Right-click one of the selected files.

3 Choose Properties from the shortcut menu.

4 Turn on the Read-Only check box.

5 Click OK.

Ideas Properties

General | Summary | Statistics

Ideas

Type: Microsoft Word Document
Location: Common
Size: 11.5KB (11,776 bytes)

MS-DOS name: IDEAS.DOC
Created: Monday, December 23, 1996 1:10:42 PM
Modified: Friday, December 27, 1996 1:11:24 PM
Accessed: Friday, December 27, 1996

Attributes: **4** ☑ Read-only   ☐ Hidden
                  ☑ Archive   ☐ System

5   OK   Cancel   Apply

10

Sharing Folders with Individuals

When you set up your computer for *user-level access control*, you can share folders with individuals, or with the entire network if you so desire. You use the names stored on your main network server to specify which individual has what type of access.

SEE ALSO

"Select the Type of Sharing" on page 173 for information about setting up your computer for user-level access control.

TIP

Different network systems use different naming services, so your access list might look different from the one shown in the dialog box at the right. The examples here are based on using a Microsoft Windows NT Server 4.0.

Share a Folder

1. Locate the folder you want to share.

2. Right-click the folder and choose Sharing from the shortcut menu.

3. On the Sharing tab, click the Shared As option.

4. Type a name for the folder.

5. Type a comment if you want one.

6. Click the Add button.

Specify the Access

1. Select the individuals or groups whom you want to have read-only access.

2. Click the Read Only button to add them to the list.

3. Select the individuals or groups whom you want to have full access.

4. Click the Full Access button to add them to the list.

Customize the Access

1 Select the individuals or groups whom you want to have customized access.

2 Click the Custom button to add them to the list.

3 Click OK.

4 Specify the types of access.

5 Click OK.

Individualize the Access

1 Select an individual whose access you want to modify.

2 Click the Edit button.

3 Change the access specifications in the Change Access Rights dialog box, and click OK.

4 Click OK.

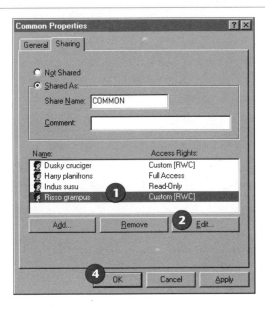

Sharing a Printer

You can set up your computer so that you can share your printer with other people in your workgroup. However, be warned that this is a situation in which you need a generous and even-tempered personality; when several people are using your printer, you'll find that your computer becomes quite sluggish.

SEE ALSO

"Connecting to a Network Printer" on the facing page for information about setting up a network printer on your computer.

Share Your Printer

1 Click the Start button, point to Settings, and choose Printers from the submenu.

2 Right-click the printer you want to share, and choose Sharing from the shortcut menu.

3 Click the Shared As option.

4 Type a name for the printer.

5 Type a comment if you want one.

6 Enter a password if you want to limit who may use the printer.

7 Click OK.

HP LaserJet 4 Properties

Graphics | Fonts | Device Options | PostScript
General | Details | Sharing | Paper

○ Not Shared
3 ● Shared As:

Share Name: GroupPrinter **4**

Comment: Workgroup Printer **5**

Password: **6**

7 OK | Cancel | Apply

Connecting to a Network Printer

A network printer is any printer that has been set up to be shared over a network, whether the printer is connected to one of the workgroup computers or to a printer server on a client-server network. When a printer is set up to be shared, you can easily connect to it and configure your system for that printer.

Get the Printer

1. Click the Start button, point to Settings, and choose Printers from the submenu.

2. Use Network Neighborhood or Windows Explorer to locate the computer that has the printer, and click that computer.

3. Drag the printer you want to use and drop it in your Printers folder.

4. Complete the Add Printer Wizard.

Drag the network printer from the computer it's connected to...

...to your Printers folder.

Printing from MS-DOS to a Network Printer

Many MS-DOS programs cannot normally print to a network printer; such programs are set to print to a standard printer port, such as LPT1 or COM1. However, you *can* print to a network printer from an MS-DOS program by having Windows reroute the output by "capturing" the network printer port. The MS-DOS program is tricked into "thinking" it's printing to a standard port, but its output is really being sent over the network.

TIP

When you run the Add Printer Wizard, select the option for printing from MS-DOS programs, and Windows will let you capture the port at that time.

Capture the Port

1 Click the Start button, point to Settings, and choose Printers from the submenu.

2 Right-click the printer you want to use, and choose Properties from the shortcut menu.

3 On the Details tab, click the Capture Printer Port button.

4 Select the port that the MS-DOS program "thinks" the printer is connected to.

5 Type the path to the network printer if it's not already completed.

6 Click OK.

7 Click OK.

This path should be the same as... ...this path.

Controlling Your Printing

When you send your documents to be printed on a network printer, each print job is *queued* in the order in which it's received by the print server. You can see the progress of your print job in the queue, and you can temporarily suspend printing of your document, or even remove your document from the queue, if you want.

TIP

You can control the printing of your document, but you can't pause the printer itself or pause or delete other users' documents in the printer queue.

TIP

Jumping the Queue.
A network administrator can set priorities for printing jobs, so some print jobs might not be printed in the order in which they're received by the print server.

View the Queue

1. Click the Start button, point to Settings, and choose Printers from the submenu.

2. Double-click the printer you're using.

Document Name	Status	Owner	Progress	Started At
Microsoft Word - New text for.	Printing	MARIANNE...	0 bytes of 1...	7:34:10 PM 12/21/96
Microsoft Word - Ideas.doc		JERRY	11.2KB	7:35:56 PM 12/21/96
Hi again		Harry Planif...	12.0KB	7:37:09 PM 12/21/96
Microsoft Word - On Line Revi.		MARIANNE...	150KB	7:38:00 PM 12/21/96

HP LaserJet 4 — Printer Document View Help — 4 jobs in queue

Documents in the printing queue   Size of each document

Stop the Presses

1. Click your document.

2. Choose the action you want from the Document menu:

   ◆ Pause Printing, to stop your document from printing until you resume printing by choosing Pause Printing again

   ◆ Cancel Printing, to delete the document from the print queue

A paused document remains in the queue but doesn't print...
...while other documents continue to print.

Document Name	Status	Owner	Progress	Started At
Hi again	Paused	Harry Planif...	12.0KB	7:37:09 PM 12/21/96
Microsoft Word - On Line Revi.	Printing	MARIANNE...	0 bytes of 1...	7:38:00 PM 12/21/96
Microsoft Word - Advanced.doc	Paused	MARIANNE...	111KB	7:40:02 PM 12/21/96
Microsoft Word - About This B.		MARIANNE...	29.3KB	7:40:50 PM 12/21/96

HP LaserJet 4 — Printer Document View Help — 4 jobs in queue

10

Sharing a Fax Modem

If you're the only person in your workgroup who has a fax modem, and you're using Microsoft Fax, you can share your modem so that your coworkers can send faxes via your fax modem.

TIP

Make sure your modem is set to answer calls. If it isn't, your coworkers won't be able to connect to it.

SEE ALSO

"Using a Network Fax" on page 184 for information about sending faxes using a network fax server.

Share a Fax Modem

1. Click the Start button, point to Settings, and choose Control Panel from the submenu.

2. Double-click the Mail (or Mail And Fax) icon.

3. Click the Services tab, and select Microsoft Fax.

4. Click Properties.

5. Click the Modem tab.

6. Turn on the Let Other People On The Network Use My Modem To Send Faxes option.

7. If asked for the drive, specify the drive that will be used to store fax messages.

8. Click Properties.

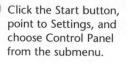

Harry Planifrons Properties

Services | Delivery | Addressing

The following information services are set up in this profile:

- Microsoft Fax
- Microsoft Mail
- Personal Address Book
- Personal Folders
- The Microsoft Network Online Service

Add... | Remove | Properties
Copy... | About...

Show Profiles...

OK | Cancel | Apply | Help

Microsoft Fax Properties

Message | Dialing | Modem | User

Select and setup the fax modem you use to send faxes.

Active fax modem: Sportster 28800 Internal

Available fax modems:

Sportster 28800 Internal

Properties...
Add...
Remove...

Set as Active Fax Modem

☑ Let other people on the network use my modem to send faxes

Share name: Fax   Properties...

OK | Cancel

If a great deal of faxing is being conducted through your computer, you'll probably experience a substantial reduction in the computer's responsiveness. If its sluggishness becomes unbearable, consider setting up a second shared modem on another computer. If that's not possible, have people schedule their faxing during the hours you're not using your computer.

"Sharing Folders with Individuals" on page 176 for information about sharing folders when you have user-level access control for sharing.

Set Up the Share

1 Turn on the Shared As option.

2 Type a name for the shared fax.

3 Add to or modify the comment.

4 Set the Access Type to Full.

5 Add a password if you want to restrict access.

6 Click OK.

7 Click OK to close the Microsoft Fax Properties dialog box.

Using a Network Fax

If a computer on your network has been set up as a network fax server, you can send faxes using that computer's fax modem.

SEE ALSO

"Sharing a Fax Modem" on page 182 for information about sharing your fax modem with your coworkers.

TIP

If you know the location of the fax share but can't connect to it, you might not have been granted access rights. Check with the owner of the fax share to gain access.

Start a New Profile

1 Click the Start button, point to Settings, choose Control Panel from the submenu, and double-click the Mail (or Mail And Fax) icon.

2 Click the Show Profiles button.

3 In the Mail dialog box, click the Add button.

4 In the Inbox Setup Wizard, specify the services you want to use, including Microsoft Fax, and click Next.

5 Type a new name for the profile, and click Next.

6 In the Microsoft Fax screen of the wizard, click Add.

7 Select Network Fax Server from the list, and click OK.

8 Type the full path to the network fax server, and click OK.

9 Enter your fax information, and complete the wizard by providing information for any other services you selected.

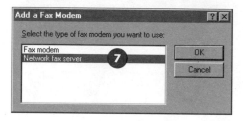

TIP

Fit the Profile? *Profiles in Windows Messaging give you a lot of versatility in the way you set up your Inbox. By defining different profiles for yourself, you can switch to different services or have your messages stored in different folders. Creating a new profile instead of extensively modifying an existing one makes things easier for you—and Windows usually responds by having fewer problems.*

SEE ALSO

"Setting Up a Computer for Different Users" on page 116 for information about creating a user profile.

"Creating Different Mail Setups" on page 238 for information about switching profiles.

Specify the Profile

1 Select the new profile as your startup profile.

2 Click Properties.

3 On the Services tab, select Microsoft Fax from the list, and click Properties.

4 Click the Modem tab, and select the network fax server.

5 Click Set As Active Fax Modem.

6 Click OK to close the Microsoft Fax Properties dialog box.

7 Click OK to close the new profile's Properties dialog box.

8 Click Close to close the Microsoft Exchange Profiles dialog box.

10

Verifying Who's Connected

If you've set up your computer to share folders with your coworkers, you can see who is connected to your computer. You can, for any legitimate reason (no, bad moods and power trips are *not* legitimate reasons), decide to "pull the plug" and disconnect someone from your computer.

TIP

If Net Watcher is not listed, you'll need to install it.

SEE ALSO

"Adding or Removing Windows Components" on page 156 for information about installing Windows components.

Start the Monitor

1 Click the Start button, point to Programs, Accessories, and System Tools, and choose Net Watcher from the submenu.

2 Choose By Connection from the View menu to see who is connected to your shared folders and from which computer.

In By Connection view, click a user's name...

...to see a list of the folders that user is connected to and which files he or she has open.

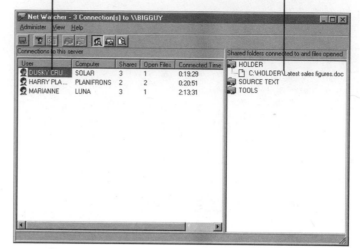

Disconnect a User

1 Click the name of the user you want to disconnect.

2 Choose Disconnect User from the Administer menu.

3 Confirm that you want to disconnect the user.

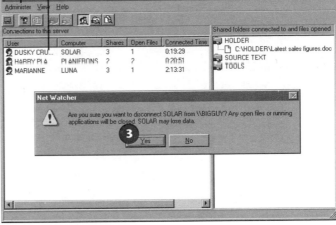

Check Your Sharing

1 Choose By Shared Folder from the View menu.

2 Click a folder to see which computers are connected to that folder.

3 Change the type of sharing for a folder by selecting it and choosing Shared Folder Properties from the Administer menu.

List of all your shared folders

Type of access set for the share

Computers that are connected to the selected folder

10

Chatting Across the Net

You can chat with other people across your network by installing Chat. To use Chat, you need to install a small communications program that is loaded when Windows starts, and then you can start Chat when you want to hold a conversation. Chat must be installed on each computer that is to be included in the chat session.

TIP

Chat isn't installed during a typical Windows 95 installation, but it is on the CD version of Windows 95. If you don't have the CD version, you can download the program from Microsoft.

SEE ALSO

"Starting a Program When Windows Starts" on page 152 for information about adding a program to the StartUp folder.

Install Chat

1. Click the Start button, point to Settings, choose Control Panel, and use the Add/Remove Programs Wizard to add Chat from the Other\Chat folder on your Windows CD.

2. Add Netdde.exe from the Windows folder to the StartUp folder of the Start menu.

3. Restart your computer.

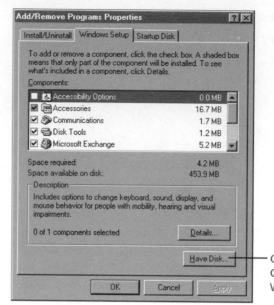

Click to install Chat from the Windows CD.

Make a Call

1. Click the Start button, point to Programs and Accessories, and choose Chat from the submenu.

2. Click the Dial button.

3. Type the name of the computer you want to connect to, and click OK.

4. Wait for the other person to answer.

5. Repeat steps 2 through 4 to add others to your conversation.

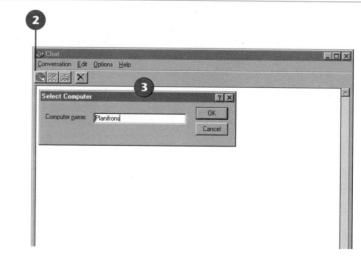

SEE ALSO

"Getting Free Software" on page 288 for information about downloading additional software from Microsoft.

TIP

You can customize the appearance of the Chat window by choosing items from the Chat window's Options menu.

TIP

If you don't feel like chatting, or if you're too busy, choose Preferences from the Chat window's Options menu, turn off the Autostart Chat When Called check box, click OK, and close the Chat window.

TIP

For more sophisticated network conferencing, Microsoft created the NetMeeting program, which is included in the Internet Explorer Startup Kit.

SEE ALSO

Section 13, "Using the Net," starting on page 245, for information about Microsoft Internet Explorer Startup Kit.

Receive a Call

1 When the phone rings on your computer, answer the call:

- ◆ Click the Chat button on the taskbar if Chat isn't running.

- ◆ Click the Answer button if Chat is running.

2 Type your text in the top part of the Chat window.

3 Read what the other people have to say in the lower parts of the window.

4 Click the Hang Up button when you've finished chatting.

4

```
Chat - [PLANIFRONS, SOLAR]
Conversation  Edit  Options  Help

I need help figuring out how to do this.

                    2

Did you look it up in a book?

Have you read that great new book, Windows 95 At A Glance?    3

Connected to PLANIFRONS, SOLAR
```

10

Changing Your Passwords

As if it's not difficult enough to remember your passwords, good security procedures—not to mention ruthless network administrators—require you to change your passwords periodically. Windows simplifies the process by letting you change several passwords at the same time.

TIP

Some networks require you to use different tools for changing your network password. If the procedures described here don't work, consult your network administrator about any special procedures for your network.

Change Your Windows Password

1 Click the Start button, point to Settings, and choose Control Panel from the submenu.

2 Double-click the Passwords icon.

3 Click the Change Windows Password button.

4 If any network password options are shown, turn them off so that you're changing only your Windows password. Click OK.

5 Type your old password, and then type a new one. Type the new password again to confirm it, and click OK.

6 Click OK.

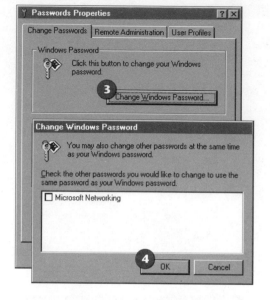

Change Your Network Password

1 Click the Change Other Passwords button.

2 Select the network access for which you want to change your password.

3 Click the Change button.

4 Type your old password, and then type a new one. Type the new password again to confirm it, and click OK.

5 Click OK when Windows confirms the change.

6 Click Close.

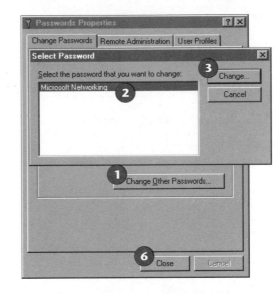

Logging On Only Once

When you start a computer that's connected to a network, you're usually asked for your network password and then your Windows password. Why not simplify your life by using the same password for both? Then you can log on to your network and to Windows with a single entry.

Change Your Passwords

1 Click the Start button, point to Settings, and choose Control Panel from the submenu.

2 Double-click the Passwords icon.

3 Click the Change Windows Password button.

4 Select your network, and click OK.

5 Type your current Windows password.

6 Type and confirm a new password, and click OK.

7 Type your current network password, and click OK.

8 Click OK when Windows confirms the change.

9 Click Close to close the Password Properties dialog box.

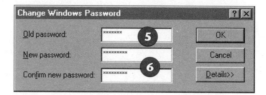

Using Mail, Fax, and Phone

When you think about communicating with other people via your computer, you're likely to be thinking about *e-mail,* or electronic mail. That's what some of this section of the book is about: setting up your Inbox so that you can send, receive, and forward e-mail. But there's a lot more to communicating than sending e-mail. You can send enclosures with your e-mail: documents, pictures—even sound and video clips. You don't need to go out and buy a fax machine, because you can use your computer to send and receive faxes. You can even write one message and send it to some people as a fax and to others as e-mail. And you can use your Inbox with online services and Internet service providers.

This section also shows you how to create and administer a post office for sending and receiving mail within your workgroup. If you have a modem, you can set up a HyperTerminal so that you can connect to bulletin boards or other types of terminal services, and transfer files between computers. You can even use your modem with an accessory program called Phone Dialer to place telephone calls for you.

Windows 95 is updated frequently, so some of your Inbox components might look a little different from the illustrations you see in this section.

Setting Up the Inbox

When Windows 95 was installed on your computer, it placed an Inbox on your Desktop. However, before you can use the Inbox to send and receive mail and faxes, you have to be set up with a mail system, whether it's a workgroup post office, a network mail server, or an online service.

SEE ALSO

Section 15, "Taking Care of Problems," starting on page 275 if you need further help when you're setting up your Inbox.

TIP

Gather up the information you need before you start the Inbox Setup Wizard. If you're connecting to a mail service on your network, ask the mail administrator for the procedures, locations, and passwords you'll need.

Specify Your Services

1 Double-click the Inbox on your Desktop.

2 Select the services you want to use.

3 Step through the wizard, providing information on each service you want. When you've finished, the Inbox opens.

The Inbox Setup Wizard will set up each service you select.

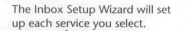
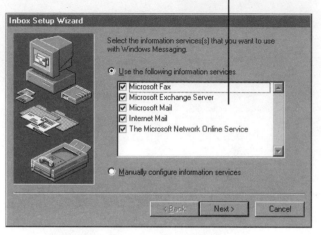

Set the Defaults

1 Choose Options from the Tools menu, and click the Send tab.

2 Click the Font button, and set the default font, font size, and color you want to use.

3 Make any other changes you want to the default settings.

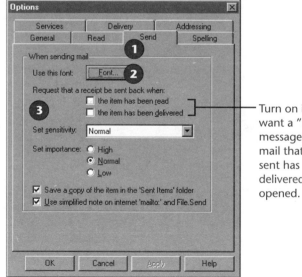

Turn on if you want a "receipt" message when mail that you've sent has been delivered or opened.

The Inbox doesn't have its own spelling dictionary, so the Spelling tab is active only if you have a spelling checker installed from Microsoft Office or from another Microsoft 32-bit program.

Turn On the Spelling Checker

 Click the Spelling tab.

2 Turn on the spelling checking options.

3 Turn on any other spelling options you want.

4 Click OK.

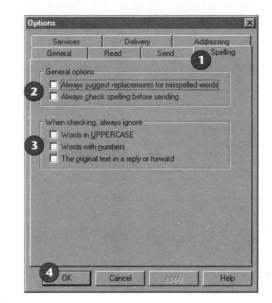

Sending E-Mail

Creating and sending an e-mail message is faster, easier, and more convenient than sending a letter through the U.S. Postal Service. You don't have to write an envelope, lick a stamp, or trek to the mailbox on a cold, rainy day. All you do is select a name, create a message, and click a Send button. Your Inbox and your mail server do the rest. What a great idea!

SEE ALSO

"Using an Online Service for Mail" on page 208 for information about transmitting sent messages to an online service provider.

"Using Microsoft Word in E-Mail" on page 216 for information about composing mail using WordMail.

Address a Message

1 Click the New Message button.

2 Click the To button.

3 Select the address list you want to use.

4 Select the name of the person you're sending mail to.

5 Click the To button.

6 Select the name of someone you want to receive a copy of the mail.

7 Click the CC button.

8 Repeat steps 4 through 7 to add other recipients to this mail.

9 Click OK when you've included everyone you want.

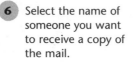

Compose a Message

1 Click in the Subject box, type a subject, and press Tab to move into the message area.

2 Type your message, applying any formatting you want from the Formatting toolbar.

3 Click a button on the toolbar to set delivery options:

◆ Click Read Receipt to be notified when the message is opened by the recipient.

◆ Click Importance: High to mark the mail with a High Importance tag.

◆ Click Importance: Low to mark the mail with a Low Importance tag.

4 Click the Send button to send the document.

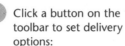

Reading E-Mail

Windows lets you know when you receive new mail, and you can specify the type of notification you prefer. You can check your Inbox and see at a glance which messages haven't been read, and you can browse through them in order or open them selectively.

TIP

You need to set the notification options only once. Whichever options you choose, a little envelope icon appears on the Windows taskbar when you receive new mail. When you double-click the icon, your Inbox becomes the active program on your Desktop.

Set the Notification

1 Choose Options from the Tools menu to display the Options dialog box.

2 On the General tab, select the type of notification you want each time new mail arrives:

◆ Play A Sound, if you want to hear a sound

◆ Briefly Change The Pointer, to have the mouse pointer change into an incoming-letter icon for a moment

◆ Display A Notification Message, to have a dialog box appear and stay open until you click a button

3 Click OK.

Options — 1

Services	Delivery	Addressing
General	Read	Send	Spelling

When new mail arrives
- ☑ Play a sound — 2
- ☑ Briefly change the pointer
- ☐ Display a notification message

Deleting items
- ☑ Warn before permanently deleting items
- ☑ Empty the 'Deleted Items' folder upon exiting

When starting Windows Messaging
- ○ Prompt for a profile to be used
- ⊙ Always use this profile:
  - Harry Planifrons

☑ Show ToolTips
☑ When selecting, automatically select entire word

3 [OK] [Cancel] [Apply] [Help]

SEE ALSO

"Associating a Sound with an Event" on page 84 for information about setting a custom sound for the New Mail Notification.

TIP

Unopened messages are displayed in bold type in the Inbox window. A folder that contains unread messages is also displayed in bold type.

TIP

You can minimize the Inbox window after you've read your mail, and simply click the taskbar button to open the Inbox window the next time you want to read your mail.

TIP

The Inbox has two views: one shows the contents of the selected mail folder, and the other shows the names of the different mail folders. Click the Show/Hide Folder List button to switch between views.

Read Your Messages

1. Open the Inbox folder if it's not already open.

2. Double-click an unread message.

3. Read the message.

4. Click the Next or Previous button to look through the other mail in your Inbox.

5. Close the Messaging window when you've read your mail.

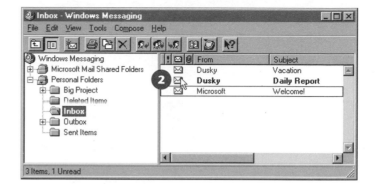

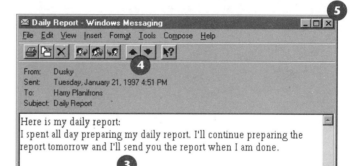

Replying to E-Mail

When you receive an e-mail message that needs a reply, all it takes is a click of a button to create a reply window that's already addressed for you. You can also have the reply window contain a copy of the original message so that the response will contain a complete record of the conversation.

TIP

You set the formatting for the original text only once; the Inbox will use those settings until you change them.

Format the Original Message

1 Choose Options from the Tools menu, and click the Read tab.

2 Specify the way you want original messages to be treated when you reply to them.

3 Click the Font button to set the appearance of the text in your reply.

4 Click OK.

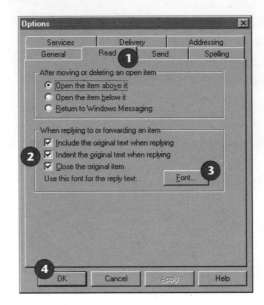

Reply to the Message

1 Open the message you
want to respond to.

2 Click the appropriate
reply button:

◆ Reply To Sender,
to send your reply
to the writer of the
message only

◆ Reply To All, to
send your reply to
the writer of the
message *and* every-
one listed in the
original message's
To and CC lines

3 Add names to or delete
names from the To and
CC lines.

4 Type your reply.

5 Click the Send button.

The reply message is
addressed automatically.

The original subject line is
included. *RE* indicates that
this is a reply.

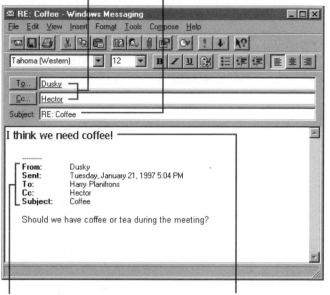

The original header information
and message text are included
and indented.

The text you type
uses your standard
reply-font formatting.

11

Forwarding E-Mail

Message forwarding is a great convenience: you can forward any e-mail message that you've received to one person or to many people. Or, if you've sent an original message to several people and then realized that you've left someone out, you can forward that message to the person you forgot—with your apologies, of course.

TIP

When you forward a single message, it's sent as a message. When you forward several messages, however, they become mail objects within a single message. To read each message, double-click it.

Forward a Message

1 Open the message you want to forward to someone.

2 Click the Forward button.

3 Insert the recipients' names in the To and CC lines.

4 Type your message.

5 Click the Send button.

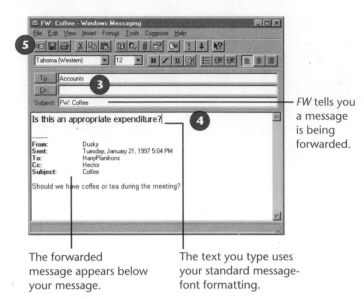

FW tells you a message is being forwarded.

The forwarded message appears below your message.

The text you type uses your standard message-font formatting.

Forward Several Messages

1 Select the messages to be forwarded.

2 Click the Forward button.

3 Insert the recipients' names in the To and CC lines of the new message window.

4 Type your message.

5 Click the Send button.

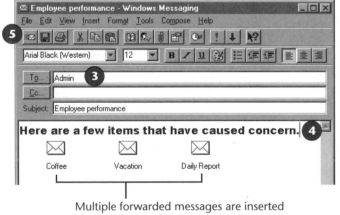

Multiple forwarded messages are inserted as message attachments. Recipient double-clicks each icon to open the message.

Mailing a File

You can send an entire file—a Word document, a sound file, a text file, or a collection of files—by including it in a mail message as an attachment. When you send the message, the attached file is sent as an object and is usually shown as an icon in your mail text. The recipient can double-click the icon to open the attachment, or right-click it to save it as a file.

Include a File

1. Create and address a message.

2. Type the message text.

3. Click the Insert File button.

4. Use the Insert File dialog box to find and select the file to be included.

5. Verify that the An Attachment option is selected.

6. Click OK. The file's icon appears in your message.

7. Click the Send button.

Creating a Folder System

The Inbox comes with the basic folders you need for managing your e-mail, and you can then create as many folders and subfolders as you need to organize and store your mail messages. You can also customize your Inbox window so that the columns in the right side of the window display the information you want to see at a glance when you're scanning the listings in your mail folders. You can change the number of columns that are displayed in the window, the order in which they appear, and their width.

Create a Folder System

1. Click the Show/Hide Folder List button if the folder list isn't displayed.

2. Click Personal Folders.

3. Choose New Folder from the File menu, type a name for a new folder, and click OK.

4. Click other folders, and repeat step 3 to create additional subfolders.

5. Drag messages from one folder and drop them into a different folder to organize them.

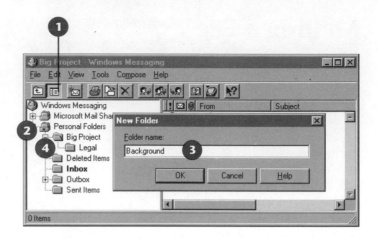

Customize a Folder

1 Click a folder whose appearance you want to modify in the right side of your window, where the information about your messages is displayed.

2 Choose Columns from the View menu to display the Columns dialog box.

3 Modify the columns in the folder:

- ◆ Add new items.
- ◆ Remove current items.
- ◆ Change the order of the items.
- ◆ Change the width of each column.

4 Click OK.

Columns in the selected folder are changed and re-ordered.

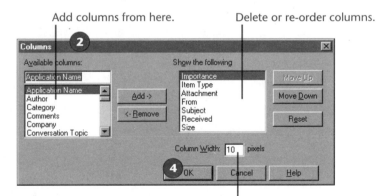

Add columns from here.

Delete or re-order columns.

Specify the width of the selected column.

Adding an Address to an Address Book

When you use e-mail, you don't need to type an address every time you send a message; you can retrieve addresses from one of your address lists. You might want to copy an address you use frequently from your company-wide address book into your Personal Address Book for quick reference.

TIP

Some additional information, such as phone numbers or office room numbers, might be displayed next to the names in your Personal Address Book. To look at all the information that's listed, select the individual's name, and click the Properties button.

Add an Address

1 Click the Address Book button on the Inbox toolbar.

2 Select the address list that contains the name you want to add to your personal address list.

3 Locate and select the name you want to add.

4 Click the Add To Personal Address Book button.

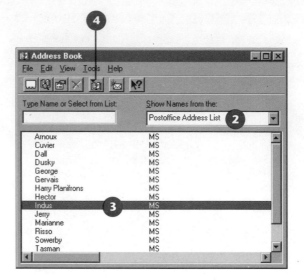

Create a New Address

1. Click the New Entry button on the Address Book toolbar.

2. Select the address book in which you want the name to be stored.

3. Double-click the type of address you're adding.

4. Fill in the address information.

5. On the tabs, fill in any additional information you'll want to refer to.

6. Click OK.

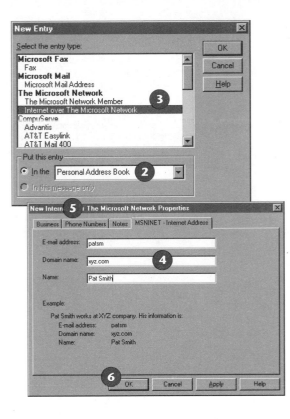

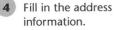

Add an Address from a Message

1. Open the message.

2. In the message header, right-click the name you want to add.

3. Choose Add To Personal Address Book from the shortcut menu.

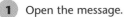
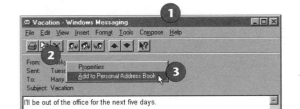

11

Using an Online Service for Mail

The Inbox works with many online services—The Microsoft Network, CompuServe, and many Internet service providers—and it can save you considerable connect-time costs if you dial in to the service only to send and retrieve your mail rather than remaining connected for long periods of time. You simply add the service to your list of messaging services, and compose and read your messages off line.

TIP

The Microsoft Network (MSN) is automatically added to your listing of online services when you set it up. Contact your Internet service provider (ISP) for information about connecting to the service using your Inbox.

Send Your Messages

1 Address and create a mail message.

2 Click the Send button.

3 Repeat steps 1 and 2 for any other messages you want to send.

4 Point to Deliver Now Using on the Tools menu, and choose the service you want to use from the submenu.

5 If a sign-in screen appears, complete the information to connect to your service provider.

6 Wait while all your messages are sent and any new messages are retrieved.

7 Check your Inbox folder for new messages.

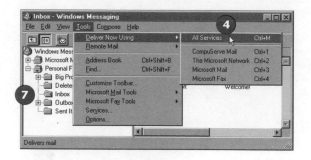

Using Your Inbox with CompuServe

CompuServe has its own program that you can use to connect and to send and retrieve mail. But you can use the Inbox to connect to CompuServe automatically. When you're ready to send and receive mail, you connect to the service and, when your messages have been sent and any new mail has been received, you disconnect from the service and read the new messages off line.

SEE ALSO

"Getting Free Software" on page 288 for information about getting drivers if you don't have the CD-ROM version of Windows 95.

TIP

CompuServe—like many other service providers—updates its software fairly frequently. Check with the service for the most recent release.

Set Up CompuServe

1 Use Windows Explorer to navigate to the Drivers\Other\Exchange\ Compusrv folder on your Windows CD.

2 Double-click the Setup program.

3 Install CompuServe Mail as one of your default settings.

4 Complete the Inbox Setup Wizard, providing your CompuServe information.

5 Close your Inbox, and then restart it.

6 Point to Deliver Now Using on the Tools menu, and choose CompuServe Mail from the submenu.

If you leave the Password box blank, you'll be asked for your password each time you connect.

CompuServe Mail connects without a startup window.

Sending a Fax

If your computer has a fax modem or if your network or mail system has a fax server, and in either situation you have Microsoft Fax installed, you can send faxes directly from your computer to another computer or to a fax machine.

SEE ALSO

"Sharing a Fax Modem" on page 182 for information about installing Microsoft Fax if it's not already installed.

"Using a Network Fax" on page 184 for information about connecting to a network fax server.

Set Up Your Faxing

1 Open your Inbox if it's not already open.

2 Point to Microsoft Fax Tools on the Tools menu, and choose Options from the submenu.

3 On the Message tab, specify the send options you want:

- When you want the fax to be sent

- Whether you want to include a cover page

- Which design you want for the cover page

4 On the User tab, fill in any missing information that should be included on the fax cover page.

5 Click OK.

Setting a time to send holds all your faxes in the fax queue until the specified time.

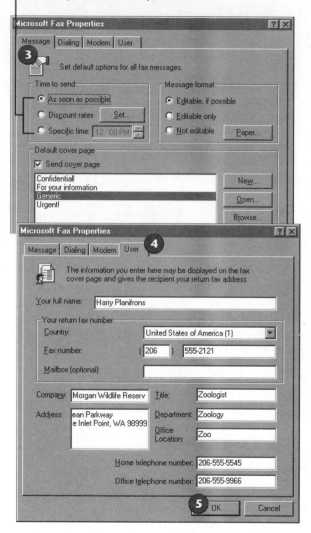

"Creating a Fax Cover Page" on page 213 for information about modifying a fax cover page.

TIP

After you complete the fax, Microsoft Fax will take a while to process the information and create the fax before sending it.

TIP

If you're not going to include a cover page with your fax, make sure that the first page of the document contains the name 'of the person you're sending the fax to, as well as your name, fax number, and telephone number for callback if there are any problems when you're sending the fax.

Send a Fax

1 Choose New Fax from the Compose menu. The Compose New Fax Wizard starts.

2 Add the recipients' addresses.

3 Specify whether you want a cover page included and, if so, which one.

4 Type a subject for the fax, and add a note if necessary.

5 Add any files you want to include:

   ◆ A file is received as an object when it's included in a fax with an editable format and received by a computer with Microsoft Fax installed.

   ◆ The contents of a file are printed, if possible, when it's included in a fax with a non-editable format or sent to a fax machine.

6 Click Finish to send the fax.

Type a name and fax number...

...or click here, and choose a fax address from your address book.

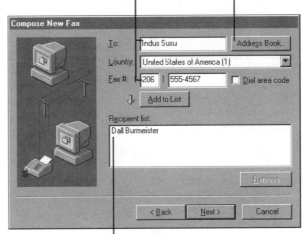

Everyone listed here will receive the fax.

Your default choice for the cover page is shown, but you can change it.

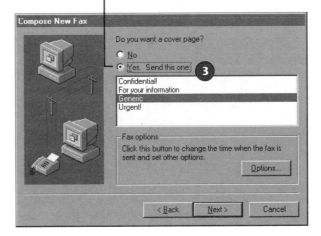

Sending Faxes and E-Mail from One Message

You can create a single message and send it to both fax and e-mail recipients. You indicate to the Inbox which type of message you want to send by the type of address you use—if it's an e-mail address, the message will be sent as an e-mail message, and if it's a fax address, the message will be sent as a fax.

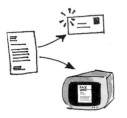

Create a Message

1. Click the New Message button.

2. Click the To button.

3. Add existing fax and e-mail addresses to the To and CC lines.

4. Click the New button to create a fax address if necessary.

5. Double-click Fax.

6. Complete the fax address information.

7. Click the To button.

8. Type the fax message. Include any files you want to send.

9. Click the Send button.

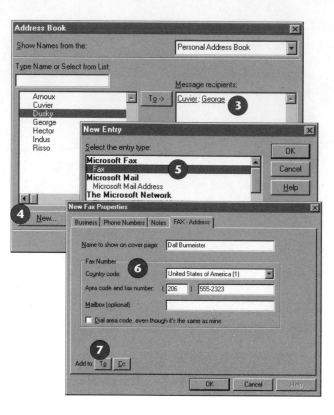

Creating a Fax Cover Page

When you send a fax using Microsoft Fax, you can include a cover page that merges data from your address book with your own user information (which you supplied when you set up your fax services). Microsoft Fax comes with four cover-page styles, which you can modify to your own design using the Fax Cover Page Editor program.

TIP

The Fax Cover Page Editor works just like most drawing-editing programs, except for the inclusion of the data fields. You can stack and group items, and you can even use the area at the right of the page as a scrap area for storing items that you don't necessarily want to include on every cover page.

Modify a Cover Page

1 In the Inbox, point to Microsoft Fax Tools on the Tools menu, and choose Options from the submenu.

2 On the Message tab, select the cover page you want to modify, and click the Open button.

3 In the Fax Cover Page Editor program, choose Save As from the File menu, and save the file under a different filename.

4 Modify the cover page as desired:

 ◆ Delete any elements you don't want.

 ◆ Use the Drawing tools to add visual elements.

 ◆ Use the Insert menu to add data fields that insert information about the sender, the recipient, or the message.

 ◆ Use the Alignment tools to arrange the elements.

5 Click the Save button.

6 Choose Exit from the File menu.

Selection tool

Text tool

Drawing tools

Alignment tools

Data fields are replaced with information you have supplied.

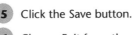

Select several elements by dragging the Selection tool over them, and then position them using the Alignment tools.

Drag an existing data field into a new position or delete it. Add a new data field using the Insert menu.

11

Receiving a Fax

If your computer is equipped with a fax modem, you can set the computer to receive faxes automatically, to receive faxes only when you tell the computer to answer incoming calls, or to disregard incoming calls while still maintaining your ability to send faxes.

Set the Answer Mode

1 Open your Inbox if it's not already open.

2 Point to Microsoft Fax Tools on the Tools menu, and choose Options from the submenu.

3 On the Modem tab, select your fax modem, and click Properties.

4 Select the Answer mode you want.

5 Click OK.

6 Click OK to close the Microsoft Fax Properties dialog box.

7 Close and restart the Inbox.

If you select the manual answer mode, you'll be prompted each time the phone rings.

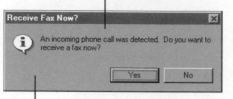

Select if you want your computer to answer the phone whenever it rings.

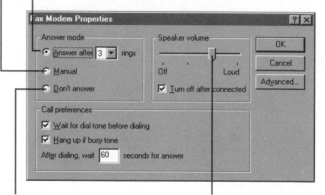

Select if you don't want your computer to answer any calls.

Set to Off if you don't want to hear your modem screeching while it's connecting.

A fax is stored in a special graphical format, not as text. Although you can copy a portion of a fax and paste it into WordPad, it is still a picture and you can't edit or format its "text."

Open a fax. Display the thumbnails, and click the thumbnail of a page that contains information or images that you want to use. Adjust the zoom control, and drag the page so that the information you want is visible. Click the Select button, drag a selection rectangle around the material, and choose Copy from the Edit menu. Start Paint, and choose Paste from the Edit menu. Edit the content as you would any bitmap.

View a Fax

1 Double-click the fax message in your Inbox folder. The Fax Viewer displays the message.

2 Use the toolbar buttons to view or print the fax.

3 Choose Exit And Return To Windows Messaging.

4 If you made changes, choose Yes to save them or No to discard them.

Turn on to change your view of the fax by dragging it.

Turn on to show a thumbnail image of the fax.

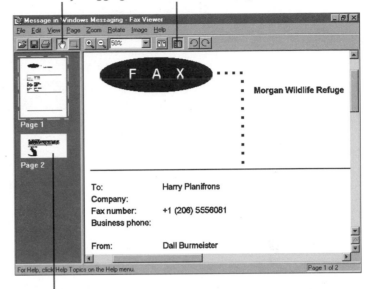

Click a thumbnail to jump to that page.

Using Microsoft Word in E-Mail

If you have Microsoft Word 95 or later on your computer, you can use WordMail as your e-mail editor. WordMail lets you use Word's powerful features—formatting, spelling and grammar checking, AutoFormat, AutoText, and so on—in your e-mail messages.

> **TIP**
>
> *WordMail must be installed on your computer if you want to use it as your e-mail editor. If you don't see the WordMail Options on the Inbox's Compose menu, rerun Word Setup and install WordMail.*

> **TIP**
>
> *You can use any font in an e-mail message, but if the recipient's computer doesn't have the same font installed, your message will be displayed in a default font.*

Turn On WordMail

1. In the Inbox, choose WordMail Options from the Compose menu.

2. Turn on the Enable Word As E-Mail Editor option.

3. Click the template you want to use.

4. Click the Close button.

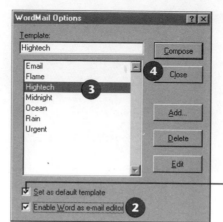

Turn on if you want to use the selected template for all your messages.

Compose a Message

1. Click the New Message button.

2. Address your message, and add the subject line.

3. Compose your mail, using any of Word's tools.

4. Click the Send button.

Mailing tools are included on Word's toolbar.

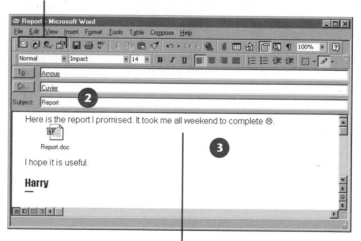

Use Word's tools—including AutoFormat, AutoCorrect, AutoComplete, spelling and grammar checking, tables, and different views—to complete your message.

Read a Message

1 Double-click a message.

2 If the message isn't formatted, click the AutoFormat button.

3 Close the WordMail window when you've finished reading the message.

Plain-text message

Click the AutoFormat button to format text.

Click to hide mail header information.

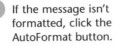

Bullets replace asterisks.

Formatted message

Line-breaking is corrected.

Network, Internet, and intranet addresses become hyperlinks.

Headings are formatted.

11

Setting Up Workgroup Mail

Windows 95 comes with a version of Microsoft Mail that works with your Inbox so that you can create and send mail within your workgroup. To use workgroup mail, you create a post office in a location that is shared with all the people in the workgroup.

SEE ALSO

"Creating Different Mail Setups" on page 238 for information about creating your own profile.

TIP

Make a note of the password and mailbox names for your post office, and keep the note in a secure place. If you forget either name, you won't be able to administer the post office and you'll be stuck with the job of deleting the existing workgroup post office and creating a new one.

Create a Post Office

1. Create a shared folder that allows full access to everyone in your workgroup.

2. Click the Start button, point to Settings, and choose Control Panel from the submenu.

3. Double-click the Microsoft Mail Postoffice icon. The Microsoft Workgroup Postoffice Admin Wizard starts.

4. Select the Create A New Workgroup Postoffice option, and click Next.

5. Specify the shared folder you created for the post office.

6. Enter all the administrator information.

7. Complete the wizard.

For a small workgroup, use your own name and mailbox and tell everyone to contact you for administrative support.

Enter Your Administrator Account Details	
Name:	Harry Planifrons
Mailbox:	HarryP
Password:	PASSWORD
Phone #1:	555-2323
Phone #2:	555-9898
Office:	Zoo101
Department:	Zoology
Notes:	

[OK] [Cancel]

For a large workgroup, create an administrator's mailbox, and create a new profile to log on as the administrator.

Enter Your Administrator Account Details	
Name:	ZooGroupAdmin
Mailbox:	ZooGroup
Password:	PASSWORD
Phone #1:	555-2323
Phone #2:	555-9898
Office:	Zoo101
Department:	Zoology
Notes:	

[OK] [Cancel]

TRY THIS

If someone in the workgroup forgets his or her mail password, use the Workgroup Postoffice Admin Wizard to open the post office, select the name of the person who forgot the password, click the Details button, and type a new password. After closing the wizard, give the forgetful person his or her new password (but don't e-mail it!).

TIP

Each user you add to the post office gets an individual mailbox. The mailbox name must be unique within that post office.

Administer!

1 Click the Start button, point to Settings, and choose Control Panel from the submenu.

2 Double-click the Microsoft Mail Postoffice icon.

3 Select the Administer An Existing Workgroup Postoffice option, specify the location of the post office on your computer, and click Next.

4 Enter your mailbox and password, and click Next.

All individual mailboxes are placed in the administrator's mailbox.

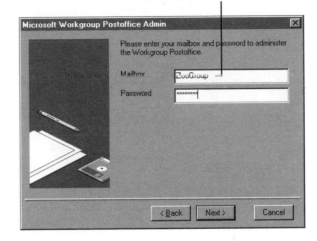

Add a New User

1 Click the Add User button.

2 Enter a user name.

3 Enter a unique mailbox name for the post office.

4 Enter a password of up to eight characters.

5 Enter any other information that you want to appear in the post office address book.

6 Click OK, and then click Close to close the Postoffice Manager dialog box.

Connecting with a Terminal

When you need to connect by modem with a terminal—a bulletin board, for example—you can do so using HyperTerminal. Hyper-Terminal is a program provided by Windows 95 that lets your computer function as a terminal. And if you have problems connecting or communicating, you can modify the settings to improve the connection.

TIP

HyperTerminal comes with some preconfigured setups for various popular services. To use one of these setups, double-click the icon, and confirm and/or modify the connection information, if necessary.

Set Up Your Terminal

1 Click the Start button, point to Programs and then Accessories, and choose HyperTerminal from the submenu.

2 Double-click the Hypertrm icon.

3 Type an identifying name for the connection, select an icon, and click OK.

4 Enter your phone information, and click OK.

5 Click the Dial button.

6 Use the sign-on information you've been assigned, and verify that the information is being displayed correctly.

7 Sign off, and click the Disconnect button.

Scroll up to see text that has scrolled off the window. Text from previous sessions is also shown.

Click to disconnect.

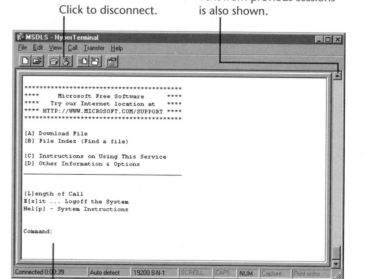

Follow the directions of the host terminal.

SEE ALSO

"Transferring Files by Modem" on page 222 for information about transferring files directly between computers.

TIP

Your connection to another computer doesn't have to be a modem connection. To connect two computers by cable, choose the correct COM port from the Connect Using list in the Phone Number dialog box that appears when you're setting up HyperTerminal.

Modify the Connection

1. Click the Properties button on the HyperTerminal toolbar.

2. On the Settings tab, click the ASCII Setup button.

3. Modify the settings as shown in the table, below right.

4. Click OK.

5. Click OK.

6. Choose Save from the File menu.

7. Try your connection again.

ASCII Setup

ASCII Sending
- Send line ends with line feeds
- Echo typed characters locally
- Line delay: 0 milliseconds.
- Character delay: 0 milliseconds.

ASCII Receiving
- Append line feeds to incoming line ends
- Force incoming data to 7-bit ASCII
- ☑ Wrap lines that exceed terminal width

OK   Cancel

MSDLS Properties

Phone Number | Settings

Function, arrow
- ○ Terminal ke

Emulation:
Auto detect

Backscroll buffer li
500

- Beep three ti

ASCII Setup...

OK   Cancel

CONNECTION-SETTING TROUBLESHOOTING	
If you have this problem	**Make this setting**
Text you send is in one long line.	Turn on the Send Line Ends With Line Feeds option.
You don't see what you send.	Turn on the Echo Typed Characters Locally option.
Some of the text you send isn't received.	Enter 1 for Line Delay. Increase the value if necessary.
Some of the characters you send drop out.	Enter 1 for Character Delay. Increase the value if necessary
Text you receive is in one long line.	Turn on the Append Line Feeds To Incoming Line Ends option.
Text you receive is garbled.	Turn on the Force Incoming Data To 7-Bit ASCII option.
The ends of lines are not visible.	Turn on the Wrap Lines That Exceed Terminal Width option.

11

Transferring Files by Modem

If you want to transfer files directly between computers via modem, you can transfer files the old-fashioned way—that is, from terminal to terminal. There is no limitation to file size, and you'll probably get the maximum speed from your modem. You can even use this method to transfer data between different types of computers, including mainframes and computers that aren't running Windows, provided the other computer has a modem and communications software. However, the procedure described here assumes that both computers are using HyperTerminal.

SEE ALSO

"Connecting with a Terminal" on page 220 for information about setting up a Hyper-Terminal connection.

Set Up the Terminals

1. On the host computer, create a new Hyper-Terminal setup, using any phone number (the number won't be used).

2. Click the Cancel button instead of dialing.

3. Click the Properties button on the toolbar, and click the ASCII Setup button on the Settings tab.

4. Turn on the Send Line Ends With Line Feeds and Echo Typed Characters Locally options.

5. Click OK.

6. Click OK.

7. On the connecting computer, set up HyperTerminal to dial the host computer, using the same ASCII Setup settings on both computers.

8. Save the settings on both computers.

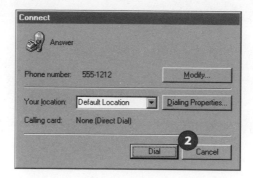

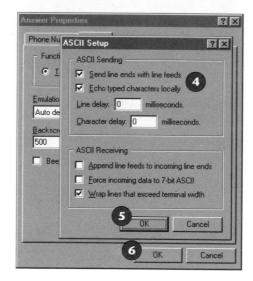

Connect the Computers

1 On the connecting computer, click the Connect button and then the Dial button.

2 When the phone rings on the receiving computer, type your modem's answer code, and press Enter. On many modems this code is *ATA*.

3 Type messages to each other to coordinate the transfer.

4 On the computer that will receive the file, click the Receive button on the HyperTerminal toolbar, specify the folder and protocol for the file, and click Receive.

5 On the computer that's sending the file, click the Send button on the HyperTerminal toolbar, locate the file, and click Send.

6 Wait for the file to be sent.

7 Click the Disconnect button when you've finished.

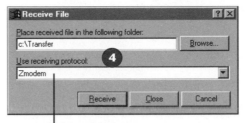

Use the same protocol on both computers.

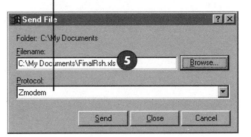

The status of the file transfer is displayed. Both computers receive the status information.

11

Making a Phone Call

If you have a telephone connected to your modem, you can use a Windows accessory program called Phone Dialer to place the call for you. You can automate the process even further by using Speed Dial buttons.

TIP

If Phone Dialer is not listed on the Accessories submenu, you'll need to install it.

SEE ALSO

"Adding or Removing Windows Components" on page 156 for information about installing Windows components.

Dial a Number

1. Click the Start button, point to Programs and then Accessories, and choose Phone Dialer from the submenu.

2. Type the number or click the buttons to enter the number.

3. Click Dial.

4. When prompted, pick up the phone and click the Talk button.

5. When the conversation is over, hang up the phone.

The number you type or enter by clicking the number buttons is shown here.

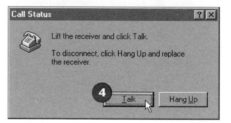

TIP

To change the name and number of a speed-dial button, choose Speed Dial from the Edit menu.

TIP

You don't have to duplicate the phone numbers that are already stored in your Address Book—you can make phone calls directly from the Address Book. Here's how: open the Address Book from your Inbox, and double-click the name of the person or company you want to call. On the Phone Numbers or the Business tab, click the Dial button for the number you want to call.

Speed It Up

1. Click a blank Speed Dial button.

2. Type a name for the button.

3. Enter the phone number.

4. Click Save.

5. Repeat steps 1 through 4 to add or change speed-dial numbers.

6. Click a Speed Dial button to call that number.

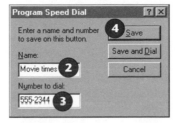

12

Being Mobile

If your work involves traveling, read this section before you take off! If you use different computers at different locations, or if you have a desktop computer at work and you travel with a notebook computer, this section of the book will help you avoid the pesky problems that can occur when you're working long distance.

You'll find out how to create one or more virtual Briefcases, into which you can stuff a bunch of files from your main computer. You can work on the files on the road, and then update them on your main computer with a mouse-click or two. If you want to take some e-mail messages with you for reference, you can transfer them to a mail folder and include them in the Inbox of another computer. You can even send and receive e-mail automatically wherever you happen to be.

If you have a portable computer with a docking station, you'll find the information in this section useful. However, we haven't gone into any details about using a docking station, simply because Windows usually detects whether a computer is docked or undocked and uses the appropriate settings by automatically switching hardware profiles. To quote the oh-so-famous words of the world's software engineers, if you have a problem, "it's a hardware problem," so check with the maker of the computer system for a fix.

Using the Briefcase to Manage Files

When your work travels with you, whether it's from your office to your home or to the other side of the world, you often need to take copies of files from your main desktop computer and use them on a different computer. If you've done this a lot, and you're aware of how difficult it can be to keep track of the most recently changed version of a file, you're going to like the Windows Briefcase. Okay, so it's not made of fine Corinthian leather. You won't care when you see how easily you can synchronize the changes you make in your traveling files with the originals on your main computer.

Copy the Briefcase onto a Floppy Disk

1. Right-click the Desktop, point to New, and choose Briefcase from the shortcut menu. Give the new Briefcase a descriptive name.

2. Drag a file or folder onto the new Briefcase icon.

3. If a welcome screen appears the first time you use the Briefcase, click the Finish button.

4. On the Desktop, right-click the Briefcase and send it to a floppy disk.

Dragging a file onto the Briefcase copies the file into the Briefcase.

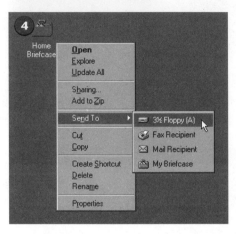

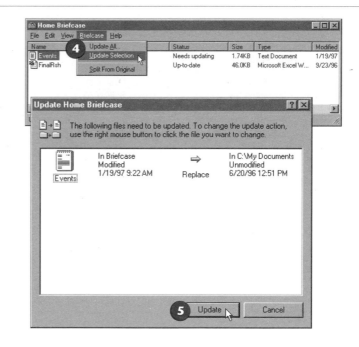

TIP

If the Briefcase isn't listed, and you don't see the My Briefcase icon on your Desktop, the Briefcase hasn't been installed and you'll need to install it.

SEE ALSO

"Adding or Removing Windows Components" on page 156 for information about installing Windows components.

TIP

If you're copying the Briefcase onto a floppy disk, the contents of the Briefcase shouldn't be greater than the capacity of the disk—usually 1.44 megabytes.

TIP

Once you've copied a file into the Briefcase, don't move or change the original file. If you do, the file in the Briefcase will become an "orphan," and you won't be able to update the original file from the file in the Briefcase. If you have orphaned your Briefcase file, you'll need to save it using a different filename.

Use the Briefcase Files

1 Insert the floppy disk into your other computer, drag the Briefcase from the disk onto the Desktop, and double-click the Briefcase icon.

2 Double-click a file you want to use. Work in your program, saving the file to the Briefcase. When you've finished, drag the Briefcase from the Desktop to the floppy disk.

Update the Files

1 Insert the disk into your main computer.

2 Open My Computer, open a window for the disk, and drag the Briefcase onto the Desktop.

3 Double-click the Briefcase icon.

4 To update

◆ A single file, select the file, and choose Update Selection from the Briefcase menu.

◆ All files, choose Update All.

5 Click Update to confirm the updating.

The Briefcase records the location of the original files...

...and tracks which files have been changed.

Copying Large Files into the Briefcase

If you need to copy files that are too large to fit on a floppy disk, you can copy the files over a network directly into the Briefcase. When you've finished working on the files, you can use the Briefcase to update the original files for you.

TIP

If you're using a large-volume removable storage device, such as a tape drive or a zip drive, follow the procedure for copying files onto a floppy disk.

SEE ALSO

"Using the Briefcase to Manage Files" on page 228 for information about copying files into the Briefcase and onto a floppy disk.

Get the Files

1. Using a network, a dial-up networking system, or a direct cable connection, connect to the computer that contains the files you want to copy into the Briefcase.

2. Locate a file you want to copy.

3. Drag the file onto the My Briefcase icon on your Desktop.

4. Repeat steps 2 and 3 until all files you want are in My Briefcase.

5. Work with the files.

6. When you've finished, reconnect to the computer that contains the original files, if necessary.

7. Open My Briefcase on your Desktop.

8. Choose Update All from the Briefcase menu, and confirm that you want to replace the original files.

The Briefcase provides some version control on a network, but it is no substitute for a good version-control program, especially if several people are working on the same document.

The Briefcase can hold large files, provided your computer has enough disk space.

Printing Without a Printer

When you're traveling and you're not connected to your usual printer, or if you're right there in your office but your printer is misbehaving, you can still print your documents. Well, not *exactly*. What you can do is create *print jobs*—that is, the documents stay in the printer *queue* until you and the printer are ready to print, and then the print jobs are sent to the printer as if you had been connected all the time.

TIP

If your printer isn't connected and you try to print without first taking the printing off line, Windows will alert you to the printer problems and take the printer jobs off line for you.

If there's no Work Offline command on the shortcut menu, use Pause Printing instead—it accomplishes the same thing.

Create a Print Job

1. With your computer attached to the printer you're going to use, set your document up for printing, and print a test piece to verify that the computer and the printer are working together.

2. Turn off the computer, and disconnect from the printer or from the network.

3. Click the Start button, point to Settings, and choose Printers from the submenu. Right-click the printer, and choose Work Offline from the shortcut menu.

4. Print your document as usual.

5. Double-click the printer in the Printers folder to review the print jobs in the printer queue.

6. Shut down your system when you've finished.

7. Reconnect to the printer or the network, and start Windows.

8. Right-click the printer in the Printers folder, and turn off the Work Offline option.

Windows gently reminds you that the printer is off line.

Document Name	Status	Owner	Progress	Started At
Microsoft Word - Stormy night	User Interve...	Jerry	11.4KB	10:03:06 AM 1/18/97
Microsoft Word - Company Man...	User Interve...	Jerry	2.24MB	11:16:43 AM 1/18/97
Final.xls	User Interve...	Jerry	66.1KB	2:26:06 PM 1/18/97
circle	User Interve...	Jerry	987KB	2:32:28 PM 1/18/97

HP LaserJet 4 - User Intervention Required - Work Offline

Printer   Document   View   Help

4 jobs in queue

All the files you want to print are queued up, waiting until the printer is on line.

12

Taking Your Mail with You

When you're away from your office, you can take important mail messages with you. You simply copy or move the messages into a special mail folder, and then transfer the folder to your other computer.

Create a Mail Folder

1 In your Inbox on your main computer, choose Services from the Tools menu.

2 In the Services dialog box, click Add.

3 In the Add Service To Profile dialog box, select Personal Folders, and click OK.

4 In the Create/Open Personal Folders File dialog box, navigate to where you want to store the file, type a name for the file, and click Open. This creates a PST-type file, which stores the folder you want to use.

5 Set the properties for the folder, and click OK.

6 Click OK to close the Services dialog box.

7 Select and drag messages from other folders into this folder. Hold down the Ctrl key while you drag if you want to copy instead of move the messages.

8 Exit and log off from the Inbox.

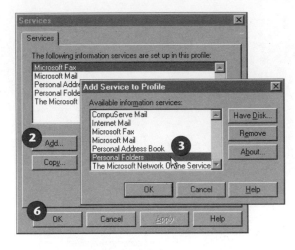

PST file is created in the Create/Open Personal Folders File dialog box.

Type a name for the folder.

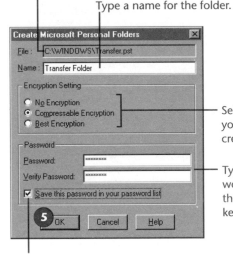

Select the level of security you want. No Encryption creates a text file.

Type and verify a password. Be sure to write the password down and keep it in a safe place.

Turn on to avoid entering your password on this computer.

SEE ALSO

*"Creating a Folder System"
on page 204 for information
about customizing the layout
of your mail folders.*

TIP

*If you're transferring your mail
to a computer that's used by
other people, create a new
Exchange profile for yourself
before you include your transfer
file. That way, you'll have your
own Inbox.*

SEE ALSO

*"Creating Different Mail
Setups" on page 238 for information about creating your
own profile.*

Transfer the Folder to Another Computer

1. Copy the PST file from where you stored it to the computer on which you want to use it.

2. In your Inbox, choose Services from the Tools menu, and click the Add button.

3. In the Add Service To Profile dialog box, select Personal Folders, and click OK.

4. In the Create/Open Personal Folders File dialog box, locate and select the PST file you copied, and click Open.

5. Type the password for the folder.

6. Set the properties for the folder, and then click OK.

7. Click OK to close the Services dialog box.

8. Retype the password if it's requested.

9. Click the new folder to review the mail.

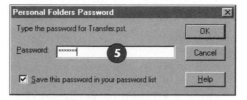

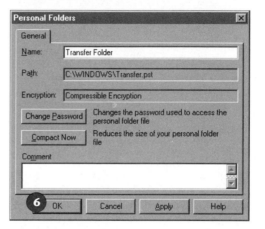

Copied mail folder with messages becomes part of the Inbox.

Receiving E-Mail from a Remote Location

If you download mail from different locations while you're traveling, you can choose not to download messages you don't want, and you can decide whether you want mail deleted from or retained on your mail server. Although different mail systems have different settings, most are really quite similar. This procedure is for setting up a connection using Microsoft Mail.

SEE ALSO

"Connecting to Your Network from a Remote Location" on page 240 for information about dial-up networking.

Set Up Remote Mail

1. In your Inbox, choose Services from the Tools menu.

2. Select the mail service that you'll be using from a remote location, and click the Properties button.

3. On the Connection tab, turn on the option for remote mail using a modem and dial-up networking, or the option to sense a LAN or a remote connection.

4. On the Remote Configuration tab, turn on the remote mail option.

5. On the Remote Session tab, turn on the options you want for the mail session.

6. Click OK, and then click OK to close the Services dialog box.

7. Exit and log off from your Inbox.

Turn on to connect to the service automatically when the Inbox is first started.

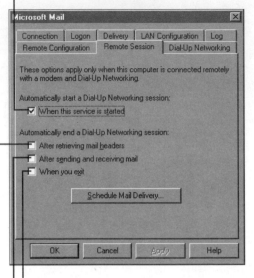

Turn on to disconnect from the service when you exit from the Inbox.

Turn on to disconnect from the service after all new mail has been received and all mail in your Outbox has been sent.

Turn on to disconnect from the service after remote mail has retrieved the latest mail headers.

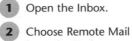
TIP

If the service you selected doesn't provide a tab for setting remote options, either the service doesn't support remote mail or you don't have Dial-Up Networking installed. Check with your system administrator if you have problems using remote mail.

TIP

If more than one service is set for remote mail, point to Remote Mail on the Tools menu. The services will be listed on the Remote Mail submenu.

TIP

Unmarked message headers are retained in the Remote Mail window, and no action is performed until you mark the header for the action you want.

Connect

1. Open the Inbox.

2. Choose Remote Mail from the Tools menu.

3. Click the Connect button.

4. Turn on the options you want, and click OK.

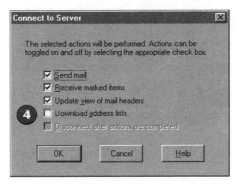

Send and Receive Mail Messages

1. Mark your message headers for the actions you want.

2. Click the Connect button.

3. Specify what you want to be sent and retrieved, and click OK.

4. Check your Inbox for delivered messages.

Marks message to be downloaded and deleted from the server.

Marks message to be downloaded and for a copy to be retained on the server.

Marks message to be deleted from the server without being downloaded.

Scheduling Remote Mail Delivery

If you're set up to use remote mail when you're away from your office, you can have your computer automatically dial in to your mail server at set intervals, connect to your network, and send and receive mail for you. Why do it yourself when Windows can do it for you?

TIP

You can schedule more than one remote mail delivery by clicking the Add button again.

Set Up an Automatic Connection

1 Exit and log off if your Inbox is open.

2 In the Control Panel, double-click the Mail (or Mail And Fax) icon. On the Services tab, click the service you'll be using from a remote location, and click the Properties button.

3 On the Remote Session tab, click the Schedule Mail Delivery button.

4 In the Scheduled Remote Mail Delivery dialog box, click Add.

5 Specify the dial-up connection.

6 Specify the interval.

7 Click OK four times to close all the dialog boxes.

8 Open your Inbox.

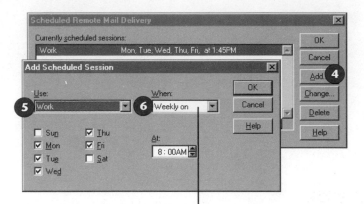

Select Every to specify a time interval between connections, select Weekly On to specify the days and the time for the connection to be made, or select Once At to specify a single date and time for the connection to be made.

Connecting from Different Locations

If you travel around a lot—breakfast in New York, lunch in Chicago, and dinner in Seattle, perhaps—and you dial in or send faxes from your computer from each location, you need to tell Windows where you're calling from so that it can use the correct dialing properties for that location.

TIP

Many modem-based services, such as Microsoft Fax and HyperTerminal, have buttons or menu commands that take you directly to the Dialing Properties dialog box.

Create a New Location

1. Click the Start button, point to Settings, and choose Control Panel from the submenu.

2. Double-click the Modems icon.

3. In the Modem Properties dialog box, click the Dialing Properties button.

4. Click the New button, type a name for the location, and click OK.

5. Specify the settings for this calling location.

Set Up a Calling Card

1. Turn on the Dial Using Calling Card option.

2. Select the calling card you want to use.

3. Enter your calling-card number.

4. Click OK.

5. Click OK to close the Dialing Properties dialog box.

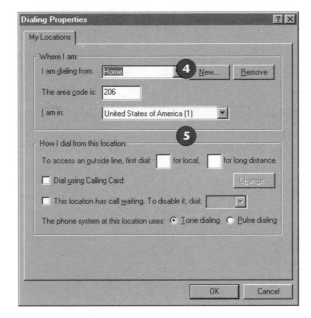

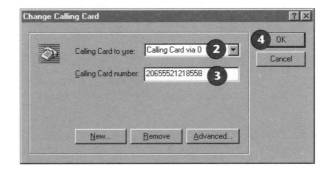

12

Creating Different Mail Setups

If you have different mail configurations available to you depending on where you are—a network fax, your own modem, a network mail server, or a remote service—you can create a different profile for each and switch to the appropriate one when you start up Exchange.

Create a Profile

1 Exit and log off from your Inbox.

2 Click the Start button, point to Settings, and choose Control Panel from the submenu.

3 Double-click the Mail (or Mail And Fax) icon.

4 Click the Show Profiles button.

5 Click the Add button.

6 Step through the Inbox Setup Wizard, specifying the services and settings for the new profile. Type a name for the profile.

7 Select the profile you want to use.

8 Click the Close button.

TIP

If none of the profiles in the Choose Profile dialog box is appropriate, click the New button and create a new profile.

TIP

If you want to adjust each service every time you start the Inbox, click the Options button in the Choose Profile dialog box, and turn on the Show Logon Screens For All Information Services check box.

Switch Your Profile

1. Open your Inbox, and choose Options from the Tools menu.

2. On the General tab, turn on the option to be prompted for a profile when Windows Messaging starts up.

3. Click OK.

4. Exit and log off from your Inbox.

5. Reopen the Inbox.

6. Select the profile you want to use.

7. Click OK.

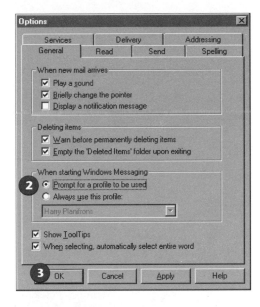

12

Connecting to Your Network from a Remote Location

If your network has dial-up network services, and you have been granted permission to connect from a remote location, you can establish a dial-up connection to your network and connect to it by phone. Once you're connected, you have access to your network just as if you were in the office.

TIP

The network administrator can restrict your access to a single computer when you dial in, or can give you full access to the entire network.

Set Up Your Computer

1 If you're using a computer that isn't normally connected to the network, configure it exactly as if it were connected to the network, using the same network protocols, computer name, workgroup name, and domain name if any, and your logon passwords.

2 Open My Computer and double-click Dial-Up Networking.

3 Double-click Make New Connection.

4 Step through the Make New Connection Wizard, typing a name for the connection and a phone number for the computer.

Use a descriptive name for the connection.

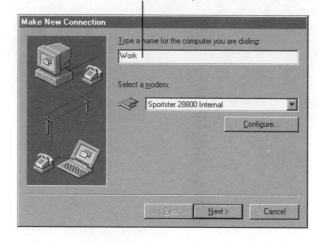

Type the number of the direct line to the server's modem.

TIP

Contact the network adminis-trator before you try to connect. He or she will be able to supply you with all the network-configuration information and the passwords so that you can log on to the dial-up server and the network. Use the Network icon in the Control Panel to configure the network settings.

SEE ALSO

"Calling to Your Computer" on page 267 for information about setting up your own com-puter as a dial-up server.

TIP

Dial-Up Networking is useful for more than just connecting to your corporate network. You can use Dial-Up Networking to connect to services such as MSN, as well as when you're connecting two computers with a direct cable connection.

Connect to the Network

1 If you haven't already logged on to your computer as if you were connecting to the network, restart Windows and log on.

2 In the Dial-Up Networking folder, double-click the con-nection you created.

3 Type your password to connect to the dial-in server, and verify the phone number and your dialing location.

4 Click Connect.

5 Wait for the connection to be made.

6 Provide any passwords required.

7 Work on the network as usual.

8 When you've finished, use your network's standard logoff proce-dure, if one is required.

9 Click the Disconnect button.

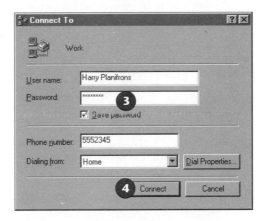

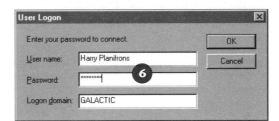

12

Connecting Two Computers with a Cable

If you want to transfer information between two computers that are not normally connected—your notebook computer and your desktop computer, for example—you can connect them using a cable that links their serial ports or their parallel ports. The cable creates a network connection between the two computers, with one computer *hosting* the other. The connection can also give the *guest* computer access to the entire network through the host computer's connections. The guest computer cannot, however, access a network that uses only the TCP/IP network protocol.

SEE ALSO

"Sharing Folders Using Passwords" on page 174 and "Sharing Folders with Individuals" on page 176 for information about sharing folders.

Connect the Computers

1. Configure the computer that will be the guest to have at least one of the same network protocols as the host computer.

2. Connect the cables.

3. On each computer, click the Start button, point to Programs and then to Accessories, and choose Direct Cable Connection from the submenu.

4. On each computer, step through the Direct Cable Connection Wizard. Specify the port to which the cable is connected on each computer.

5. Complete the steps of the wizard, and wait for the connection to be established.

Designate your main computer as the host.　　Designate the other computer as the guest.

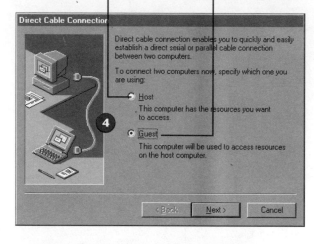

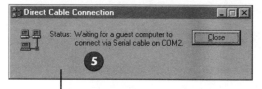

After you've completed the steps of the wizard, the host computer listens and waits for the guest computer to connect.

The fastest way to transfer information between computers is with a parallel connection, but it can sometimes be difficult to find the right kind of cable. For a parallel connection, you can use a standard 4-bit cable, an Extended Capabilities Port (ECP) cable, or a Universal Cable Module cable. The ECP cable can be used only on computers that have ECP parallel ports. The serial connection is made with an RS-232 null-modem cable.

For the direct cable connection to work, both computers must have the direct cable connection and dial-up networking features installed. The two computers must also have at least one common network protocol installed. To check the network protocols used on the host computer, double-click the Network icon in the Control Panel, and look at the listing on the Configuration tab. Click Cancel when you have the information you need. If you're not sure how to install protocols, you'll find the information in Windows Help.

Exchange Information

1 Use standard techniques to navigate through folders, and to move, copy, or delete folders or files. (Note that when you connect two computers, you have access to the other computer's shared folders only.)

- Open any of the shared folders from the host computer.

- Explore any network connections to which the guest computer is granted access through the host computer.

- Use the host computer's Network Neighborhood to explore any shared folders on the guest computer.

2 On the guest computer, click Direct Cable Connection on the taskbar, and click Close to disconnect.

3 On the host computer, click Direct Cable Connection on the taskbar, and click Close to end the direct cable connection session.

When the guest computer connects...

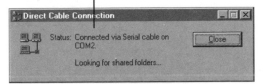

...the host computer's shared folders are displayed on the guest computer.

12

Using the Net

What is "the net," and what can it do for you? Those are big questions, to which there are many answers that fill many books. Briefly (*very* briefly!), the net is two main things: it's the Internet, where you can wander around the world accessing information about everything imaginable, and it's your company intranet—a communications system set up on a corporate network.

What can the net do for you? Whatever you want it to do—more than we can possibly describe here. But we can help you explore some of the tools that Microsoft has made available for your travels on the net.

With the most recent releases of Windows 95, Microsoft has included the Internet Explorer Startup Kit. This kit, which is also available as a separate product, contains a large array of tools—including Internet Explorer 3.0, which serves as an interface to the net—and many of these tools work whether you're using the Internet or your corporate intranet. (Most of the tools can also be downloaded from Microsoft Web sites.)

Using Internet Explorer and all its tools is a subject for an entire book. Our purpose here is to get you comfortable with basic operations and confident enough to go out and enjoy your explorations.

Going to a Net Site

To Internet Explorer, the only differences between the Internet and a company intranet are the connection and the type of address you use to connect. In either case, you can go directly to a specific site—provided you have its address or a shortcut to it—or you can "surf" the net, gathering the information you need.

SEE ALSO

"Changing Internet Explorer Links" on page 248 for information about changing the destinations of the buttons on the Links toolbar.

"Returning to Your Favorite Sites" on page 250 for information about saving addresses for future use.

TIP

If you've copied an Internet address from a document to the Windows Clipboard, you can paste the address into the Address box—just click in the box and press Ctrl+V.

Jump to a Site

1. Start Internet Explorer, and connect to the Internet if you're not already connected.

2. If the toolbar isn't displayed, choose Toolbar from the View menu.

3. Click the Links toolbar if it's not fully displayed.

4. Click a button to go to a site.

Click to display the hidden Links toolbar.

The Links toolbar contains links to several locations.

Use an Address

1. Click the Address toolbar.

2. Click the current address to select it, and insert the address you want to go to. (If you're using an intranet whose network has a gateway to the Internet, jumps from your intranet might take you to the Internet without your being aware of it. Use the Back button or the drop-down list on the Address toolbar to return to your intranet.)

3. Press Enter.

Click to display the hidden Address toolbar.

When you enter this address... ...you go to this site.

Provided they have been rated, you can use the Content Advisor to block access to sites that contain too much sex, nudity, or violence for your taste. To start the Content Advisor, choose Options from the View menu, and click the Settings button on the Security tab.

If you access the Internet from a corporate network that uses a proxy server, the network administrator can block your access to certain sites and can even record the sites you visit.

If Internet Explorer is not set up to start at your intranet home page, type the name of the intranet server in the Address box. To go to a computer that's using the Personal Web Server to publish pages on the intranet, type that computer's name in the Address box.

Surf the Net

1 From your current page, do any of the following:

- ◆ Click the Search button, and use a service to locate a site by name or location.

- ◆ Click a relevant jump on the page to go to a new site.

- ◆ Click the Back button to return to a previous site.

- ◆ Click the Forward button to return to a site you left using the Back button.

- ◆ Open the Address list to select and jump to a previously visited site.

- ◆ Click the Stop button to stop downloading a page, and then jump to a different location.

2 If you get lost, click the Home button to return to your start page, or click the Search button to conduct another search.

Move backward and forward through sites you've already visited.

Find sites that fit your search criteria.

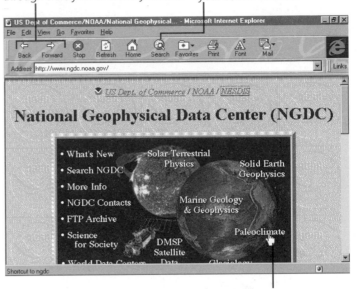

When the mouse pointer changes into a tiny hand, it's pointing to a jump that will take you to a different location.

Changing Internet Explorer Links

When you install Microsoft Internet Explorer, it has a preinstalled start page and it already contains links to other pages. Depending on your needs, you might want to have a different Internet start page. If you're using an intranet, you might want to set the start page to the main intranet page. And by customizing the other links, you can create quick and easy access to other pages with a click of a button.

TIP

If you want to reset a button on the Links toolbar to its original destination after you've changed it, select the link on the Navigation tab, and click the Use Default button.

Set a New Start Page

1 Navigate to the page you want to use as your start page.

2 Choose Options from the View menu, and click the Navigation tab in the Options dialog box.

3 With Start Page selected, click the Use Current button.

4 Click OK.

Set New Links Destinations

1 Navigate to the page you want to use as a link.

2 Choose Options from the View menu, and click the Navigation tab in the Options dialog box.

3 Select a link. These links correspond to the buttons on the Links toolbar.

4 Type the caption you want to use to identify the button.

5 Click the Use Current button.

6 Click OK.

7 Repeat steps 1 through 6 to redefine links to other buttons.

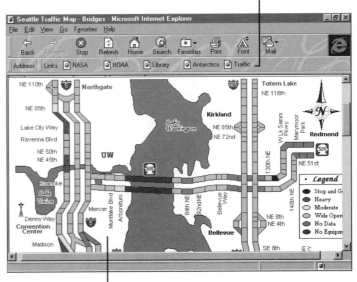

Click a redefined button...

...to go to that site.

Returning to Your Favorite Sites

When you find a good source of information or entertainment, you don't need to waste a lot of time searching for that site the next time you want to visit it. You can simply add the site to your Favorites list, and Internet Explorer obligingly creates a shortcut to the site for you.

SEE ALSO

"Sharing a Site" on the facing page for information about saving shortcuts or addresses to Internet sites.

Save a Location

1. Navigate to the site whose location you want to save.

2. Click the Favorites button on the Links toolbar, and choose Add To Favorites from the drop-down menu.

3. Type a name for the site, or use the proposed name.

4. Click OK to add the site to your Favorites folder.

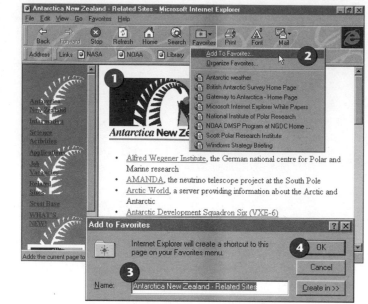

Return to a Location

1. Click the Favorites button.

2. Click the name of the site you want to return to.

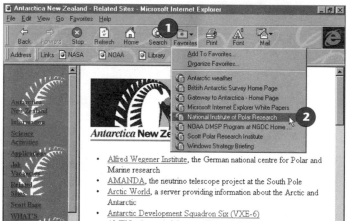

Sharing a Site

Don't keep all the good sites to yourself! You can share a great site with friends and colleagues by sending them a shortcut to the site. If you prefer, you can send the address rather than a shortcut.

TIP

Any documents created in Microsoft Office 97 programs can contain hyperlinks to Internet or intranet sites. This capability provides a very friendly and powerful way to share Web sites.

TIP

If you want to share a site that you visited fairly recently but didn't add to your Favorites folder, take a look at your History folder and see if it's listed there. Both folders are usually located in your Windows folder.

Get the Shortcut

1. Navigate to the site you want to share with someone.

2. Click the Favorites button on the toolbar, and add the site to your Favorites list.

3. Use My Computer or Windows Explorer to open your Favorites folder. Drag the shortcut to the site to copy it into an e-mail message or into any appropriate document.

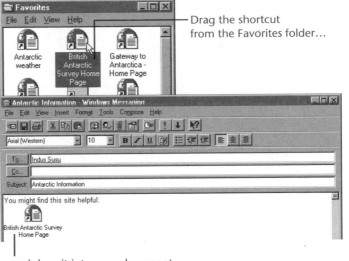

Drag the shortcut from the Favorites folder...

...and drop it into your document.

Get the Address

1. Open the Favorites folder.

2. Right-click the shortcut and choose Properties.

3. Click the Internet Shortcut tab.

4. With the Target URL text selected, press Ctrl+C to copy it.

5. Click Cancel.

6. Paste the address into your document.

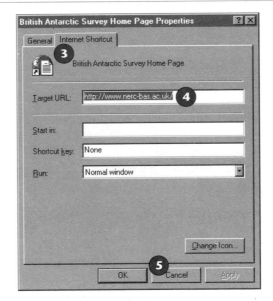

Chatting over the Internet

Microsoft Comic Chat provides an entertaining way to "chat" over the Internet. The chat must be hosted by a chat server, and your fellow chatterers need to be using Comic Chat too; otherwise, the graphics won't do much.

TIP

Mother Knows Best! *When you were little, she said, "Don't talk to strangers!" Now she says, "Don't tell strangers in chat rooms anything important about yourself!" Chat rooms often have strange characters lurking in corners. Unless you know whom you're dealing with, it's a good idea to remain anonymous.*

TIP

You can change the number of horizontal panels in the comic strip by adjusting Page Layout on the Settings tab of the Options dialog box.

Set Up Your Comic Strip

1. With Comic Chat running, choose Options from the View menu, and click the Character tab.

2. Select the character you want.

3. Click the Background tab.

4. Select a background for the comic.

5. Click the Personal Info tab.

6. Make any changes to your information.

7. Click OK.

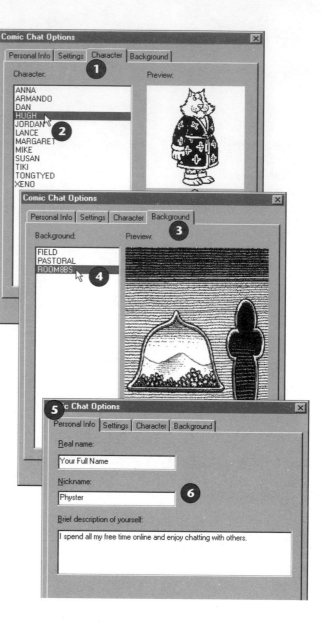

Your text can affect the gestures of your character. Either in a chat session or when you're practicing offline, start your comment with the word "I." In another comment, use "You" as the first word. Note the way your character points. If you're angry, type in all caps and you'll see that your typing can change your character's emotions. Experiment with e-mail "shorthand," such as LOL and :).

To practice working with the characters, save a Comic Chat session when you've finished chatting, disconnect, and then choose Open from the File menu. Open the saved chat session, move to the end of the chat, and then type your new dialog and adjust your character's emotions and gestures.

If the drawing of the comic strip on your screen is too slow or too distracting, or if you're the only person in the conversation who's using Comic Chat, you can turn off the graphics and view text only. To do so, choose Plain Text from the View menu.

Chat Away

1 When you're connected to the Comic Chat server, choose Chat Room List from the View menu.

2 Select a Chat Room, and click Go To.

3 Select an emotion.

4 Type your comment.

5 Click a button for the way you want your comment posted:

◆ Click Say to place your text in a voice balloon.

◆ Click Think to place your text in a thought balloon.

◆ Click Whisper to have your text sent only to the character whose name you've clicked.

◆ Click Action to display a text frame with your name and some text at the top of the panel.

Other characters participating in the chat
Your character, with selected emotion

Type your text here.   Your character with your text

Drag the dot to change your character's expression.

Reading the News

One of the components of the Internet Explorer Starter Kit is Microsoft Internet Mail And News. With it, you can connect to newsgroups from the news server provided by your Internet service provider or from news servers provided by others. When you connect to a newsgroup, you can read and post messages. When you subscribe to a newsgroup, you have the fastest and easiest access to that newsgroup.

TIP

Internet News supports offline reading and replying. You designate messages or a newsgroup to be downloaded while you're connected, and then you disconnect and review the material. Your replies are stored in the Outbox until you reconnect.

Select Your Newsgroups

1 With the News Reader connected, click Newsgroups.

2 If you have more than one news server, select the one you want to use.

3 Search for the newsgroups you want to access.

4 Double-click a newsgroup to subscribe to it. The groups to which you've subscribed will appear on the Subscribed tab and in the Newsgroups list in the Internet News window.

5 Select the newsgroup you want to visit.

6 Click Go To.

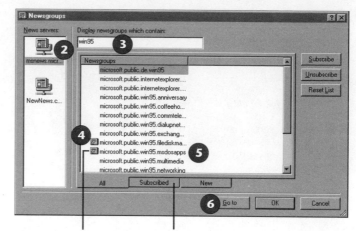

The newspaper icon shows you've subscribed to that newsgroup.

Only the newsgroups you've subscribed to are listed on the Subscribed tab.

To customize the News Reader's toolbar, right-click it and choose Customize to change the buttons, or choose Align to move the toolbar to the left side of the window.

To place the message header and the message text pane side by side, point to Preview Pane on the View menu and choose Split Vertically from the submenu.

There are many news servers on the Internet—some public and some private. To add a new news server, choose Options from the News menu, and click the Add button on the Server tab. Supply a user name and password only if they are required by the newsgroup. (You can obtain the user name and password from the server administrator.)

Read the News

1. Click the message you want to read. If you want to see the message in a whole window rather than in a pane of the News Reader, double-click the message.

2. Read the message. If you opened a separate window for the message, close the window when you've finished.

The regular font shows that the message has been read.
The Bold font shows that the message hasn't been read.
All newsgroups you've subscribed to are listed.

A plus sign means there are additional messages related to the first message. A minus sign means all the messages in the series are displayed. A series of messages is called a *thread*.

Posting a Newsgroup Message

Newsgroups are interactive—that is, you can read and reply to messages and post your own messages. When you reply to a message, you can post your response in the newsgroup or you can mail your response directly to the author of the message. You can also customize your signature and have it added automatically to your messages.

TIP

Where Did It Go? *If you post a message and then open it from the newsgroup to review it, you might not see that message the next time you go to the newsgroup. The message is still there, but you probably have your News Reader set to display unread messages only. To display your message, choose All Messages from the View menu.*

Set Up Your Response

1. With the News Reader open, choose Options from the News menu, and click the Server tab.

2. Add to or change any of your personal and contact information.

3. Click the Signature tab.

4. Click the Text option.

5. Type the signature text you want to add to your messages.

6. Select which types of message you want the signature to be added to automatically.

7. Click OK.

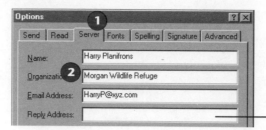

Complete if you want messages sent to an e-mail address other than the one from which you're sending your message.

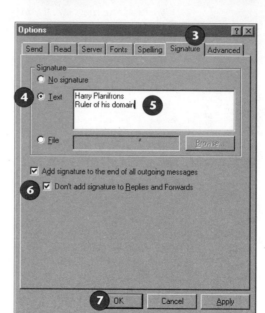

Most newsgroups have specific rules of conduct. Make sure that your messages are compatible with each newsgroup's etiquette; language or topics that are acceptable in one newsgroup might be offensive in another. Also, be cautious about creating long messages, especially when you're including text from a message you're responding to.

Post Your Message

1 Click the appropriate button:

◆ New Message to post a new message

◆ Reply To Group to post a response to the message you've selected

◆ Reply To Author to send an Internet Mail message to the author of the message you've selected

2 Type your message.

3 Click the Post Message button or the Send button.

Click, and type a subject.

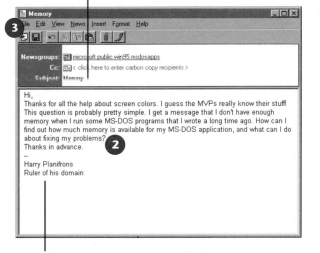

Signature is inserted automatically.

Using Internet Mail

If you're connected directly to the Internet, you can use the Internet Mail part of Internet Mail And News to send and receive messages. When your Internet mail is configured based on information provided by your Internet service provider, you can compose messages, respond to messages you've received, and forward messages.

Read Your Mail

1. With Internet Mail open and connected to the Internet, click Send And Receive.

2. Click the message you want to read.

3. Read your message.

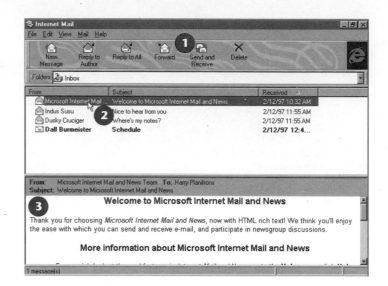

Send a Message

1. Select a message, and click the Reply To Author or Reply To All button. Or click the New Message button to create a new message.

2. Complete or modify the To, CC, and Subject lines.

3. Type your message.

4. Click the Send button.

5. Click the Send And Receive button to send all your messages and to receive any waiting messages.

Click to open your Address Book.

If you don't complete this line, it will be blank in the message.

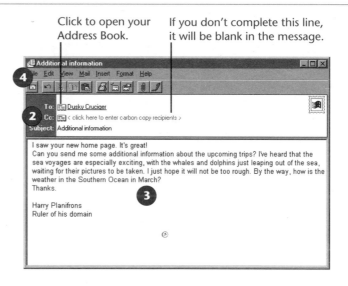

Adding On to Your System

Windows 95 isn't a static system, and there are many *add-on* features available to enhance its functionality. Two of those add-ons are Microsoft Plus! and Microsoft IntelliPoint 2.0 software.

Microsoft Plus! is a package of assorted, if somewhat unrelated, goodies: some take care of serious business and some are for fun. On the serious side is a sinister-sounding feature called System Agent that lets you set up a regular and convenient schedule for running your system's maintenance programs. You can also use System Agent to schedule programs to run while you sleep—the ultimate efficiency! And you can combine Microsoft Plus! with Dial-Up Networking to transform your computer into a dial-up server so that other people can access your computer to transfer files. On the fun side of Microsoft Plus! is a profusion of great new Desktop Themes—art, science, sports, and more—that you can use as is or mix and match to create an eclectic theme of your own.

IntelliPoint 2.0 software lets you use the newest of pointing devices: the IntelliMouse, or *wheel mouse,* with its unique little wheel and wheel button, both of which provide you with a variety of helpful features. You'll also find out how IntelliPoint 2.0 software can relieve your "mouse-finger" woes by providing alternative ways to use the mouse.

Running Automatic Maintenance

System Agent, which is included with Microsoft Plus!, is a tool that schedules maintenance programs to run automatically. When Microsoft Plus! is installed, several maintenance programs are set up automatically to ensure that your computer operates at its optimum performance level. The table on the facing page describes what the System Agent programs do.

TIP

Work While You Sleep!
Many people keep their computers running at night and schedule the maintenance programs to run while they sleep. If you turn off your computer at night, schedule the maintenance programs to run at times when you're least likely to be using the computer: at lunchtime, during scheduled weekly meetings, or at nap.time.

Schedule a Program

1 Double-click the System Agent icon on the taskbar.

2 Right-click a program.

3 Choose Change Schedule from the shortcut menu.

4 Specify when you want the program to run.

5 Click OK.

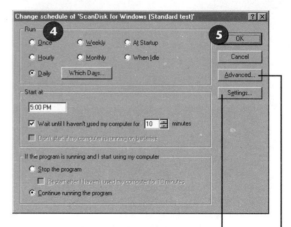

Click to customize the way the program runs.
Click to specify what to do if the program doesn't run as scheduled.

To see a record of the programs that have run, choose View Log from the Advanced menu. If the program you're interested in isn't listed, double-click the program and turn on the Log Results check box in the Properties dialog box.

"Improving Disk Performance" on page 97 for information about running Disk Defragmenter, and "Finding and Fixing Disk Errors" on page 98 for information about running ScanDisk.

If you choose the Stop Using System Agent command from the Advanced menu, System Agent won't be loaded the next time you start Windows. To reactivate System Agent, click the Start button, point your way through Programs, Accessories, and System Tools, and choose System Agent.

Turn Off a Program

1. Right-click the program.

2. Choose Disable from the shortcut menu. Choose the checked Disable command again if you want to enable the program.

3. Click the Close button to close the System Agent window but keep System Agent running in the background.

Turn Off All Programs

1. Double-click the System Agent icon on the taskbar.

2. Choose Suspend System Agent from the Advanced menu.

3. Click the Close button to close the System Agent window. The System Agent icon on the task-bar changes to remind you that it won't run scheduled programs.

SYSTEM AGENT PROGRAMS	
Program	**What it does**
Compression Agent	Compresses files to their maximum compression ratio. Available only if your disk is compressed.
Disk Defragmenter	Re-orders the items on your disk so that files are not separated into several discontiguous parts. Can take a long time to run but speeds up disk performance.
Low Disk Space Notification	Checks your hard disk to see if you're running out of free disk space.
ScanDisk For Windows (Standard)	Conducts a quick test to see if there are disk errors in any files or folders.
ScanDisk For Windows (Thorough)	Runs the standard test and also checks the disk for corrupted areas. Usually takes a long time.

To resume running programs at their scheduled times, choose the Suspend System Agent command again.

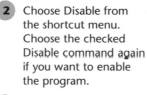

 System Agent is disabled.

Running Programs While You Sleep

System Agent will run a program when you schedule it—a convenient way to utilize your computer or the network during off hours. You need to be sure, though, that the program can run unattended and that there will be no ill effects if it's suddenly terminated.

TIP

Although you can start almost any program from System Agent, many programs don't run well unattended. If you've scheduled more than one program to run, use the Deadline settings to make sure that one program terminates before the next one starts.

Schedule a Program to Run

1 Double-click the System Agent icon on the taskbar.

2 Choose Schedule A New Program from the Program menu.

3 Click the Browse button, locate the program, and click Open.

4 Complete any additional information.

5 Click the When To Run button, and specify the time you want the program to run.

6 Click the Advanced button.

7 Specify the time you want the program to end if it hasn't terminated by itself.

8 Turn on the If The Program Is Still Running, Stop It At This Time check box.

9 Click OK to close the Advanced Options dialog box, and then click OK to close the Change Schedule dialog box.

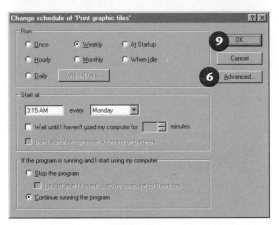

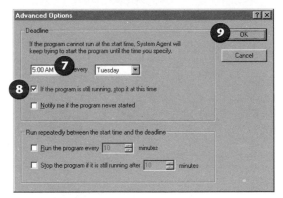

Switching Desktop Themes

With Microsoft Plus! installed, you can change the entire appearance of your computer by switching Desktop Themes. The Desktop Themes available are those you selected when you installed Microsoft Plus! You can, however, rerun Microsoft Plus! Setup and add any other themes you want from the Microsoft Plus! CD.

TIP

Although the mouse pointers in some of the themes are really nice, some make it difficult to select or to click with great precision. If you use the mouse a lot, consider turning off the Mouse Pointers option and using the default mouse pointers.

SEE ALSO

"Creating a Desktop Theme" on page 264 for information about modifying a theme and using different mouse pointers.

Switch Themes

1 Click the Start button, point to Settings, and choose Control Panel from the submenu.

2 Double-click the Desktop Themes icon.

3 Select a theme from the list.

4 Select the items to which you want to apply the changes. The window shows how your selection will affect the appearance of your screen.

5 Click the Screen Saver button to preview the screen saver.

6 Click Pointers, Sounds, Etc. to preview the mouse pointers, sound, and visual elements schemes.

7 Make sure you like the settings before you put them into effect.

8 Click OK.

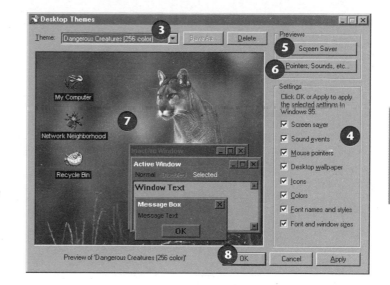

14

Creating a Desktop Theme

You're not limited to the Desktop Themes that come with Microsoft Plus! You can customize a theme to make it your own. If you create an individual theme and save your settings, you can switch to other themes and then switch back to your own creation.

TRY THIS

Select the Desktop Theme you want to use as your basis, and leave all the options checked. Close the dialog box, open it again, choose a different theme, and turn off all but the one or two features you want to apply from this theme. Close the dialog box and open it again. Choose another theme, apply one or two features, and close the dialog box. Open the Display dialog box and use the Plus! tab to change an icon. Make any other changes using the Display, Mouse, and Sounds dialog boxes. Open the Desktop Themes dialog box and save the theme.

Customize Your Settings

1. In the Control Panel, double-click Desktop Themes, apply a Desktop Theme, select the items you want from the theme, and click OK.

2. Repeat step 1 to add the elements you want from other themes.

3. In the Control Panel, double-click Display, and customize the display:

   ◆ Change the wallpaper on the Background tab.

   ◆ Change the screen saver and screen-saver settings on the Screen Saver tab.

   ◆ Change the color of any element on the Appearance tab.

   ◆ Change the icons on the Plus! tab.

4. In the Control Panel, double-click Mouse, and change any pointers.

5. In the Control Panel, double-click Sounds, and change the sounds associated with events.

Icons from the Science theme

Wallpaper from the Dangerous Creatures theme

Mouse pointer changed in the Mouse Properties dialog box

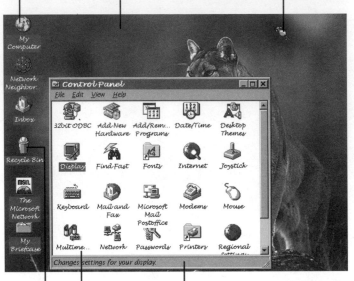

Font from The 60's USA theme

Windows colors customized on the Appearance tab

Individual icon changed using the Plus! tab

SEE ALSO

*"Changing the Look of Icons"
on page 124, "Changing
the Look of the Desktop" on
page 126, and "Changing
Screen Colors" on page 132
for information about changing the appearance of your
Desktop.*

*"Changing the Pointer Scheme"
on page 135 and "Creating a
Pointer Scheme" on page 136
for information about changing
mouse pointers.*

*"Associating a Sound with an
Event" on page 84 for information about changing sounds.*

*"Using a Screen Saver" on
page 130 for information about
changing the screen saver.*

*"Switching Desktop Themes"
on page 263 for information
about changing Desktop
Themes.*

Create a Theme

1 In the Control Panel,
double-click Desktop
Themes.

2 With Current Windows
Settings shown in the
Theme list, click Save As.

3 Type a name for
the theme.

4 Click Save.

5 Click OK.

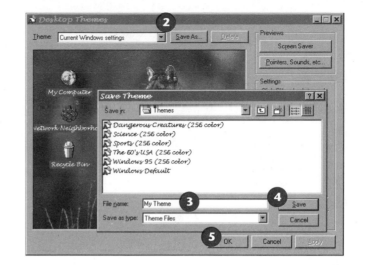

Improving the Look of Your Screen

Microsoft Plus! provides several enhancement options that can improve the look of your screen, especially if you're running at a high resolution and in High Color or True Color.

TIP

Using these enhancements requires considerable memory, so be selective. If, after applying them, you find that your computer is running slowly, turn off the enhancements one at a time until your computer's performance improves.

Turn on the Enhancements

1 Right-click in a blank part of the Desktop and choose Properties from the shortcut menu.

2 Click the Plus! tab.

3 Turn on the options you want.

4 Click OK.

Places shading around screen fonts to reduce their jagged look on the screen, but doesn't affect printed fonts.

Moves the window itself when it's being dragged, instead of showing a placeholder rectangle.

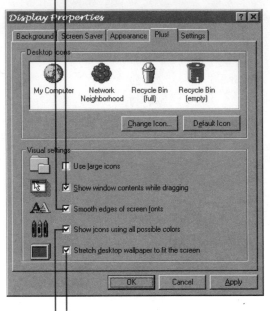

Scales a centered graphic to fill the entire screen.

Removes "dithering" from icons when system is set to High Color or True Color.

Calling to Your Computer

If you want to connect to your computer from another computer, or give access to others to facilitate file transfer between computers, you can turn your computer into a dial-up server with Microsoft Plus! and Dial-Up Networking. You control who can gain access to your computer by using a password and you can limit access to folders by setting sharing properties for the folders.

TIP

Dial-Up Networking must be installed on your computer.

SEE ALSO

"Sharing Folders Using Passwords" on page 174 and "Sharing Folders with Individuals" on page 176 for information about sharing folders.

"Connecting to Your Network from a Remote Location" on page 240 for information about dial-up networking.

Create a Server

1. Double-click My Computer.

2. Double-click Dial-Up Networking.

3. Choose Dial-Up Server from the Connections menu.

4. Turn on the Allow Caller Access option.

5. Click Change Password, type a new password, confirm it, and click OK.

6. Click Server Type.

7. Select the type of server, and click OK.

8. Click OK to start the server.

9. Provide the access number, server type, and password to the people who need the information.

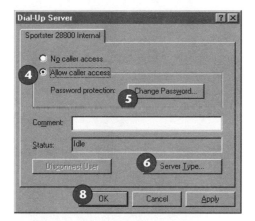

14

Scrolling with an IntelliMouse

If you have Microsoft IntelliPoint 2.0 software installed on your computer and you have a Microsoft IntelliMouse sitting on your desk, you're using the newest generation of pointing devices. Windows 95 is designed to work with the IntelliMouse, but only the most recently designed programs currently have the ability to work with the mouse's wheel. The wheel works in two ways: you can press it to use it like a mouse button and you can rotate it to use the special wheel properties.

TIP

If a program isn't designed to work with the IntelliMouse, you'll still have the full functionality of a two- or three-button mouse, but you won't be able to use the scrolling features of the wheel.

Set Up the Wheel

1 Click the Start button, point to Settings, and choose Control Panel from the submenu.

2 Double-click the Mouse icon.

3 Click the Wheel tab, and turn on the Turn On The Wheel option if it's not already checked.

4 Turn on the Turn On The Wheel Button option if it's not already checked.

5 Select Default for the button assignment if it's not already selected.

6 Click OK to close the Mouse Properties dialog box.

Click to set scrolling to a specific number of lines or to scroll one windowful at a time.

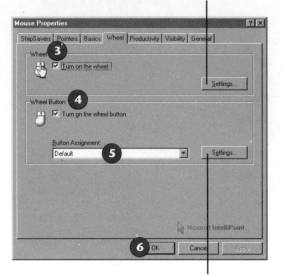

Click to set the speed of the mouse pointer when the wheel button is pressed.

From My Computer, open a folder to your Windows folder, set the display for large icons, and size the folder windows so that the horizontal and vertical scroll bars are both visible. Rotate the wheel in one direction and then in the other direction to scroll horizontally. Press the wheel and hold it down. Move the mouse to the right until the arrow points to the right and the window scrolls. With the wheel button still pressed, move the mouse in different directions and watch the way the window scrolls. Release the wheel button when you've finished playing.

My Computer windows, Windows Explorer, Internet Explorer 3.0 and later, and Microsoft Office 97 programs are all designed to work with the IntelliMouse.

Scroll a Window

1. Open a window from My Computer.

2. Place the mouse pointer over the program or window, and rotate the wheel. The program scrolls vertically by the amount you've specified.

3. Hold down the wheel and drag the mouse in the direction you want to scroll. The mouse pointer changes from a four-headed arrow into an arrow pointing in the direction you're scrolling, and the window scrolls.

4. Drag the mouse farther from its original location to increase the scrolling speed, or drag it in a different direction relative to its original position to change the direction of the scrolling.

5. Release the wheel button to stop the scrolling.

Dragging the mouse to the right scrolls the window to the right.

Dragging the mouse to the right and down scrolls the window to the right and down.

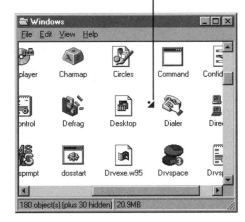

Wheeling in a Program

In Microsoft IntelliPoint 2.0 software, the functionality of both the wheel and the wheel button in the Intelli-Mouse is determined by the individual program. The wheel button functions in the same manner as a third mouse button, so if the program has features that work with a third mouse button, those features will work with the wheel button. If a program doesn't respond to the wheel button, you can change the functionality of the button. Rotating the wheel, however, is a feature unique to the IntelliMouse, so the program must be designed to work with an IntelliMouse.

Find Out What the Wheel Does

1 Read the program's documentation and online help.

2 If the information is inadequate, experiment! Try the methods shown in the table at the right and see how your program responds to the wheel action.

EXAMPLES OF USING THE WHEEL	
Action	**What it does**
Rotate the wheel.	In Word 97: scrolls up or down.
Shift+rotate the wheel.	In Windows Explorer: opens folder being pointed to or closes open folder.
Ctrl+rotate the wheel.	In Word 97: increases or decreases zoom.
Click the wheel button and move the mouse.	In Internet Explorer 3.0: scrolls in the direction the mouse is moved. Click again to turn off scrolling.
Hold down the wheel button and move the mouse.	In Windows Explorer: scrolls in the direction the mouse is moved.

Change the Wheel Button's Function

1 Click the Start button, point to Settings, and choose Control Panel from the submenu.

2 Double-click the Mouse icon.

3 On the Wheel tab, select a new function for the wheel button.

4 Click OK.

Acts as a standard third mouse button in a program.

One click is the same as a double-click of the left mouse button.

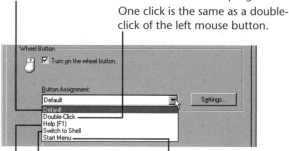

Starts Windows Explorer.

Displays context-sensitive help for the item you click.

Opens the Start menu or displays the Windows taskbar.

Hiding and Finding the Mouse

On some computer screens, or when you're running certain programs, you might find that the mouse pointer is too obvious and gets in your way. In other situations, the opposite is true—it can be frustratingly difficult to find the mouse pointer when it hides among the *t*s and *l*s in a document, for example. With Microsoft IntelliPoint 2.0 software installed, you can hide the pointer until you need it and then have it reappear with just a touch of the mouse. If you can't find the pointer on your screen, Windows Sonar will show you where it is.

Set Up the Pointer

1. Double-click the mouse icon on the taskbar.

2. Click the Visibility tab.

3. Turn on the Sonar option.

4. Turn on the Vanish option.

5. Click OK.

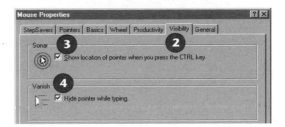

Hide and Find the Pointer

1. In a program window, start typing. The mouse pointer disappears.

2. Move the mouse to make the pointer reappear.

3. Press the Ctrl key to locate the pointer.

With the Vanish option turned on, the mouse pointer disappears when you type.

Sonar finds the mouse pointer for you.

Adjusting Mouse Movements

Microsoft IntelliPoint 2.0 software provides several options that let you customize the way the mouse works to fit your working style. You'll probably want to be a bit selective, however, in the options you use. Some are real time-savers; others can cause unexpected problems, such as the one described in the tip on the facing page. The best thing to do is turn on a few options, try them out, and decide whether or not you like them.

Speed Up Your Work

1. Click the Start button, point to Settings, and choose Control Panel from the submenu.

2. Double-click the mouse icon.

3. Click the StepSavers tab, and turn on the SnapTo, ClickSaver, and Focus options.

4. Click the Productivity tab, and turn on the ClickLock option.

5. Click the Settings button.

6. Set the duration for which the button must be held to activate the ClickLock feature, and click OK.

Positions the pointer over the default button or default item when you open a window or a dialog box. If no default is set, positions the pointer in the center of the window.

Activates a window or a dialog box when you point at the title bar instead of clicking it.

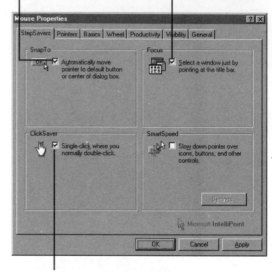

A single click acts as a double-click for items that require a double-click, but acts as a single click for items that respond only to a single click.

If you have the Windows taskbar set to Auto Hide, or if you use hidden toolbars such as the Microsoft Office toolbar set to Auto Hide, don't use the PointerWrap option. If you do, you'll become very frustrated when you want the taskbar or the toolbar to pop up! Each time you move to the bottom, top, or either side of the screen, the option causes the pointer to pop up on the opposite side of the screen instead of activating the taskbar or toolbar.

Change the Mouse Speed

1 On the StepSavers tab, turn on the SmartSpeed option.

2 Click the Settings button.

3 Adjust how much the mouse slows down when approaching an item, and click OK.

4 On the Visibility tab, turn the PointerWrap option on or off.

5 On the Basics tab, adjust the speed of the mouse pointer.

6 Click the Advanced button.

7 Specify whether, and at what rate, you want the mouse pointer to accelerate when you move the mouse quickly.

8 Click OK to close the Mouse Properties dialog box.

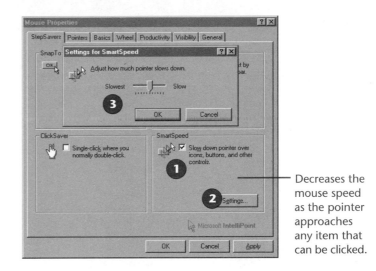

Decreases the mouse speed as the pointer approaches any item that can be clicked.

When pointer is moved off the screen, instantly moves pointer to the opposite edge of the screen.

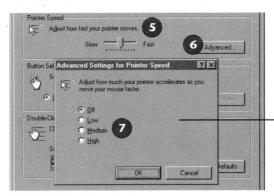

Sets how fast the pointer moves in relationship to how quickly you move the mouse.

Making Mouse Dragging Easier

Dragging items around in Windows—files between folders, text in a document, part of a picture in a drawing program, for example— is simple and convenient, but it can be hard on your "mouse finger," your wrist, and your patience. To simplify dragging, Microsoft IntelliPoint 2.0 software gives you the option of "locking" your click so that you can drag without holding down the mouse button. If you do a lot of dragging, you'll like this feature.

> **TIP**
>
> *If the pointer moves without dragging the item, hold the mouse button down longer and try again, or adjust the duration in the Settings For ClickLock dialog box.*

Turn On Dragging

1. Double-click the mouse icon on the taskbar.

2. Click the Productivity tab.

3. Turn on the ClickLock option.

4. Click the Settings button.

5. Set the length of time you need to hold down the mouse button to turn on the dragging.

6. Click OK.

7. Click OK.

Click and Drag

1. Point to the item you want to drag.

2. Hold down the left mouse button, release the mouse button, and move the mouse.

3. Move the item to where you want to drop it, and click the left mouse button.

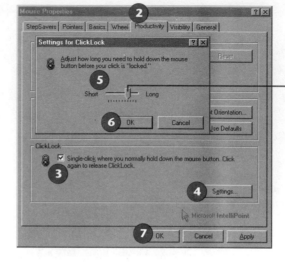

A long setting means you'll need to hold the button down for a few seconds before dragging is activated.

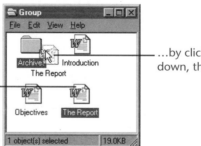

Using the ClickLock option, this document is being dragged...

...by clicking, not by holding down, the mouse button.

15

Taking Care of Problems

What if you have a problem and you can't find the information you need in this book? Although we've tried really hard to cover a broad range of problems, you still might have a question about Windows 95 that we haven't answered. If so, we'll direct you to the place where you're most likely to find an answer. Read on.

The simplest and most logical place to look for an answer is in the Windows 95 Help system (or in the Help system for a specific program if your problem is with a program rather than with Windows 95). The Windows Start button provides instant access to the Help system, and you can read the Help topics or use the Trouble-shooter to help you identify and solve your problem.

If you're still stuck, and if you have access to the Internet, you can go further afield. For example, you can visit the Windows 95 Support page, you can download the Windows 95 Support Assistant, you can search the Microsoft Knowledge Base, and you can get help from other Windows 95 users by posting your question in one of the Microsoft newsgroups. We'll show you how to find out whether you need an upgrade to your version of Windows 95 and where to get it if you do.

And maybe there's no free lunch, but there *is* free software...and we'll tell you where to get it!

Using Help to Solve Problems

The Windows 95 Help system contains many Troubleshooter topics that provide interactive support for common problems. These topics help you narrow down the possible causes for the problem you're experiencing, and in many cases they provide jumps directly to the Windows 95 dialog box in which you can fix the problem.

TIP

Many individual Help topics give you direct access to the appropriate troubleshooting topic. However, if you look up an item but don't find the information you need, see whether there's a troubleshooting entry in the Help index. For example, if you look up "modems" in the Help index, one of the many subentries is "troubleshooting."

Start the Troubleshooter

1 Click the Start button, and choose Help from the Start menu.

2 Click the Index tab.

3 Type *trouble* to display the troubleshooting topics.

4 Double-click the topic that's the most relevant to your problem.

The troubleshooting questions are arranged in a logical manner to help you diagnose your problem, but they sometimes require more information than you have, and they can lead you down a dead-end route. If you think you've chosen the wrong answer, use the Back button to backtrack, and try again. If you need to supply more information, minimize the Help window, step through the procedure that's giving you the headache, and then return to the Troubleshooter with your detailed notes in hand.

Step Through the Troubleshooter

1 Read the text, and click the option that best describes the problem.

2 Continue reading the text, taking the recommended actions, and clicking the most appropriate options.

3 Use the jump button to open the folder, dialog box, or program that will help you fix the problem.

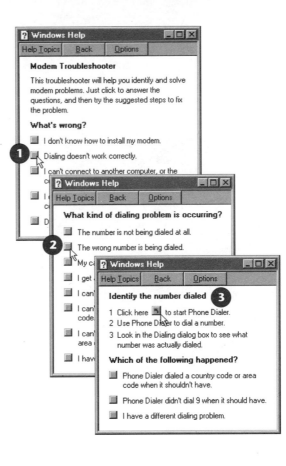

15

Finding System Information

When your system isn't working properly and you need to contact someone for help, you're going to have to supply that helpful person with some information about your system. It's quick and easy to print a listing of your system settings and to locate any devices that are misbehaving. This will be the information the support person needs. Also, if you've made changes to the system and you want to restore the original settings, you'll have them conveniently listed.

Print System Settings

1 Click the Start button, point to Settings, and choose Control Panel from the submenu.

2 Double-click the System icon.

3 Click the Device Manager tab.

4 Click the Print button.

5 With the System Summary option selected, click OK.

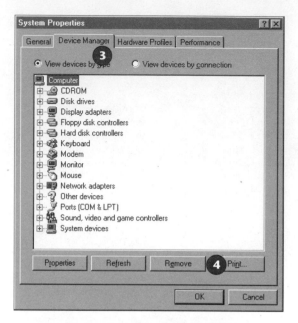

Check the Device

1 Display the information for the type of device that you think might be causing a problem.

2 Look for any symbols that seem to indicate a device isn't working or is in conflict with a resource.

3 Double-click the device.

4 Review the status information, and then click Cancel.

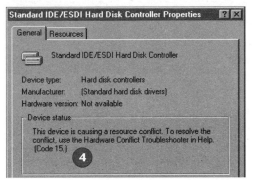

Obtaining Information from Microsoft

If you have access to the Internet, you have immediate access to a vast amount of information and product support, as well as free software, from Microsoft.

TIP

You can go directly to the Windows 95 Support page by using the address http://www.microsoft.com/ windowssupport.

TIP

Internet pages change their looks all the time, so the pages shown here might look quite different when you connect to them. It's a good idea to check the pages frequently for up-dated information.

Get Connected

1 Use an Internet browser to connect to *http://www.microsoft.com/ windows95.*

2 Click the item you want information about.

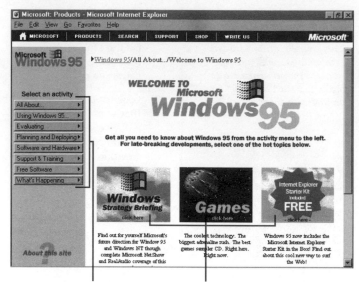

Click a button and choose an area of interest from the menu.

Click to jump to special topics.

TIP

Microsoft maintains support for all Microsoft products. To locate information about specific products, or about Microsoft itself, start at the main Web page address: http://microsoft.com.

TIP

The Support Wizard is a great tool for locating resources but, because it covers so much ground, it can sometimes be a bit frustrating. If you have any idea as to which resource might be the most helpful— Frequently Asked Questions or Downloading A Driver, for example—try that one first.

Get Support

1. Click the Support & Training button, and choose Getting Technical Support from the menu.

2. Select the Get Support Online option.

3. Use the Support Wizard to find what you need, or click one of the buttons to go directly to an item.

Click to go to a specific resource... ...or use the Support Wizard to navigate through the available sources to find the information you want.

15

Getting an Assistant

Meet the Windows 95 Support Assistant—a free tool that was developed by Microsoft support engineers. It's a powerful resource that can answer the most frequently asked questions about installing and working with Windows 95, as well as extremely technical questions on systems management. Also included with the Support Assistant are files that list hardware and software known to work correctly with Windows 95. You can download the Support Assistant from the Internet and then install it on your computer.

**Windows 95
Support Assistant**

Download the Support Assistant

1 Create an empty folder on your C: drive.

2 Use an Internet browser to connect to *http://www.microsoft.com/ windows/support/ assist.htm.*

3 Download the Assist program, saving it as a file in the folder you just created.

4 When downloading is completed, open the new folder and double-click the Assist program.

5 After all the files have been extracted, double-click the Setup program.

6 Specify whether to install the Support Assistant Help files only or to include the Hardware and/or Software Compatibility listings too.

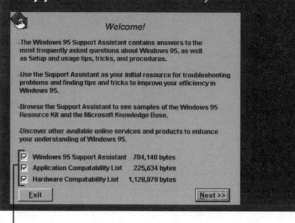

When you run the Setup program, you can select which information you want to install.

Use the Support Assistant

1 Click the Start button, point to Programs and then to Windows 95 Support Assistant, and choose Windows 95 Support Assistant from the submenu.

2 Use the Support Assistant just as you normally use Windows Help.

3 If you installed the hardware/software compatibility files, click their Help file shortcuts on the Start menu for information about program- or hardware-compatibility issues.

The Windows 95 Support Assistant is a standard Help file, filled with problem-solving information.

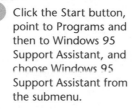

Searching the Knowledge Base

Microsoft has gathered all documented Windows 95–related problems—and, in many cases, the techniques for solving them—and placed them in the Microsoft Knowledge Base. This is the same tool that's used by Microsoft's support engineers, and it's also the "secret weapon" of many consultants. By using good keywords and a couple of search techniques, you should find the solution to most of your problems in the Knowledge Base—and it's free!

SEE ALSO

"Getting an Assistant" on page 282 for information about using the Windows 95 Support Assistant.

Access the Knowledge Base

1 Use an Internet browser to connect to *http://www.microsoft.com/kb.*

2 Select the product you want information about.

3 Type your keyword or key phrase.

4 Specify whether you want the title only or the title and a brief excerpt.

5 Click Next.

6 Review any articles relevant to your problem that are returned by the search.

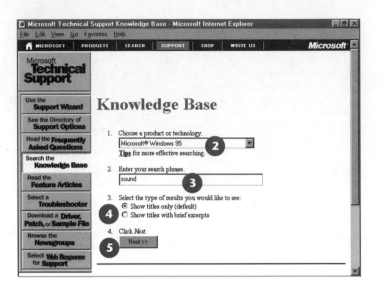

Refine the Search

1. Click the New Search button or use the Back button to return to the main search page.

2. Select the product if necessary.

3. Use more precise keywords, and use any of the operators shown in the table at the right to create a more specific search. (Replace the examples with your own keywords.)

4. Click Next.

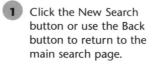

SEARCH STATEMENTS	
Statement	**What it does**
keyword1 AND *keyword2* (sound AND volume)	Finds article that includes both keywords.
keyword1 OR *keyword2* (sound OR volume)	Finds article that includes either *keyword1* or *keyword2* or both keywords.
keyword1 keyword2 (sound volume)	Finds article that includes *keyword1* followed immediately by *keyword2*.
keyword1 NEAR *keyword2* (sound NEAR volume)	Finds article in which *keyword2* occurs within 50 words of *keyword1*.
"keyphrase" ("sound and volume controls")	Finds article that contains the entire keyphrase, even if it contains operators AND, OR, or NEAR or special characters.
*startofkeyword**** (count*)	Finds article that contains words that start with the *startofkeyword* characters (country, countenance, counting).
keywordstem (sit**)	Finds article that contains any word form of the *keywordstem* (sit, sat, sitting).

15

Getting Help from Other Windows 95 Users

If the Help topics and the Microsoft Knowledge Base haven't solved your problem, there's yet another resource you can use. Microsoft maintains a series of newsgroups that are available to anyone who needs them. Microsoft doesn't support the newsgroups by having its own engineers answer questions, but there are many knowledgeable people—including an ever-expanding group of MVPs—prowling the newsgroups in search of unanswered questions.

TIP

MVPs (Most Valuable Professionals) volunteer their time to answer questions posted in the newsgroups, and are recognized by Microsoft for their expertise and efforts. They're happy to help, but they're not there to do all the work for you.

Post Your Question

1. Set your Internet newsreader to use the news server *MSNews.Microsoft.com.* If you don't have a newsreader installed, navigate to the newsgroups page *(http://www.microsoft.com/windowssupport/default-news.htm),* and download Microsoft Internet Mail and News.

2. Search for newsgroups that contain the keyword *win95.*

3. Select the newsgroup whose name seems the most relevant to your problem.

4. Go to that newsgroup.

5. Post a message with full details of the problem, including information about your system, if relevant.

6. Check back periodically for a reply. Most questions are answered within a day or two.

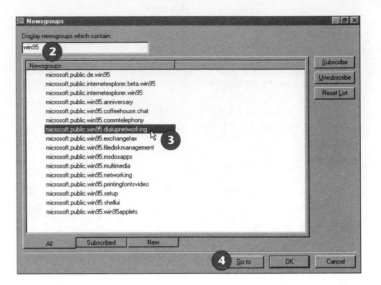

Patching Up Your System

A special service pack for early releases of the Windows 95 operating system is available from Microsoft. This service pack fixes, or *patches,* some known problems and adds a few enhancements to Windows 95, Microsoft Exchange, Microsoft Plus!, and Microsoft Internet Explorer 2.0. If you encounter any problems with your system, and the Knowledge Base or another information source suggests that you upgrade your version of Windows 95, you can download the service pack and install the programs.

SEE ALSO

"Getting Free Software" on page 288 for information about obtaining software and software patches.

See Whether You Need an Upgrade

1 Click the Start button, point to Settings, and choose Control Panel from the submenu.

2 Double-click the System icon.

3 On the General tab, look at the version number under Microsoft Windows 95. If there is a letter after the number, the system has already been upgraded.

4 Close the System Properties dialog box.

5 If there is no letter following the number, obtain and install the service pack. If your computer is fairly new and if it came with Windows 95 pre-installed, check with the manufacturer or dealer to see whether you need to install the service pack.

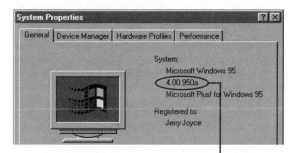

This computer has the service pack installed...

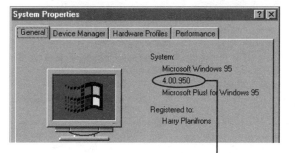

...and this computer doesn't.

15

Getting Free Software

Microsoft posts updates, fixes, add-on files, and programs that you can download from the Microsoft Internet site.

TIP

Read the download and installation instructions carefully, and follow the procedures exactly to avoid problems later.

TIP

Some software items, including most service packs, are quite large. If you're downloading using a modem, be prepared to spend a long time connected.

Download the Software

1. Create a empty folder in which to store the downloaded file.

2. Use an Internet browser to connect to *http://www.microsoft.com/ windows95.*

3. Click the Free Software button, and choose the type of software you want.

4. Navigate to find the item you want to download.

5. Read the download instructions.

6. If you're given the option, download the item as a file into your new folder.

7. Install the software as instructed on the Internet download page.

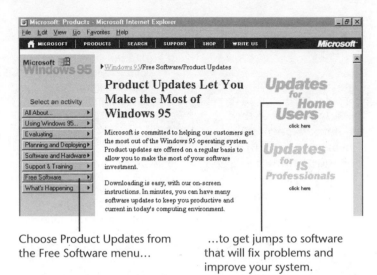

Choose Product Updates from the Free Software menu...

...to get jumps to software that will fix problems and improve your system.

Choose Shareware And Utilities from the Free Software menu...

...to get jumps to software that expands your system.

Working with Beta Software

Although the software that's available for download has usually been through an extensive and rigorous testing program, beta software is still software that's under development, and it has the potential to cause problems that run the gamut from minor to major. Whenever you use beta software, you can prevent such problems by taking a few simple precautions.

TIP

When they've finished working with beta software, many beta-software testers routinely reformat their computer's hard disk to get rid of all the junk that beta software can leave behind; then they reinstall all their software. As extreme as it sounds, this is often the best way to avoid software problems.

Install the Software

1. Back up all your files to a location external to your computer.

2. If you have an earlier version of the beta software installed, remove it.

3. Close all running programs except Windows 95, Windows Explorer, or any folder windows you have open.

4. Double-click the file to start the installation, and follow the directions on the Setup screens.

5. When the setup is completed, restart Windows.

6. Play with the program but do not use it for any work you can't afford to lose. Back up all the files from all your programs frequently. If the program causes problems, uninstall the software and wait for the next release!

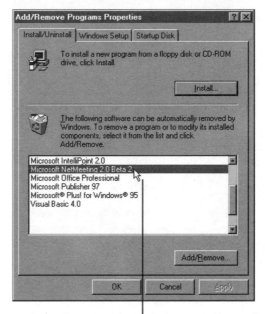

Use Add/Remove Programs in the Control Panel to remove a previous version of a software program or to remove beta software that is causing problems.

15

Looking Ahead

By now, you and Windows 95 are a team. You're getting your work done better and faster than ever before. Well, take a deep breath and get ready for some major changes!

If you want to be on technology's cutting edge, Microsoft is eager to help. Because of the increased use of the Internet and the ever-present software wars, Microsoft frequently posts prerelease, or *beta*, software on the Internet, and it's available for you to download. The advantages are that it's cutting-edge software and it's free of charge! The disadvantages are that it's beta software and it's likely to have many more bugs in it than the release software does.

The big change that's coming up in Windows 95's future is Microsoft's Internet Explorer 4.0. Although it's wrapped in secrecy because it's still under development, we do know that it will change the way your computer looks and works. Internet Explorer 4.0 is far more than an upgraded browser; it actually changes the way Windows works—and it changes the way *you* work with Windows. Internet Explorer 4.0 hadn't been released when this book went to the printer, so we aren't permitted to say very much about it—but we *were* able to sneak a quick peek to see what kinds of changes it will make to Windows 95. One of the exciting new features is the *Active Desktop,* where the most recent information about your area of interest is automatically updated throughout the day and placed directly on your Desktop. Another feature is the new *Web view* for all your folder windows and for Windows Explorer.

The Active Desktop

The Active Desktop lets your Windows 95 Desktop come alive instead of sitting there waiting to do your bidding. Once the Active Desktop is set up, it updates information without your intervention. For example, depending on your interests or needs, you might have stock quotes updated every couple of minutes or weather conditions updated every hour. Not interested in stocks, weather, sports scores, and the like? For the serious corporate environment, you can use the Active Desktop to update almost anything—inventories, sales reports, events, staff and office assignments, schedules, and so on (provided, of course, that the information is being published on the network for you to see).

Web View

Web view breaks down the barriers between surfing the Internet and surfing your computer. If you like the way you navigate on the Internet—that is, the jumps are underlined and the jumps you've used are a different color from that of unused jumps—turn on Web view. Web view also provides background images to enliven your windows, and it gives you the ability to view Internet-type documents right in your folder windows.

But the changes don't stop there—Microsoft Internet Explorer 4.0 has freed Windows 95 from so many bonds that you'll want to take the time to explore and to see how Windows 95 is getting ready to enter a new, active world.

The Active Desktop

Part of your Desktop becomes active,
ready to receive a wealth of information.

Web View

Use the toolbar buttons to navigate through your folders…

…or jump to a specific address.

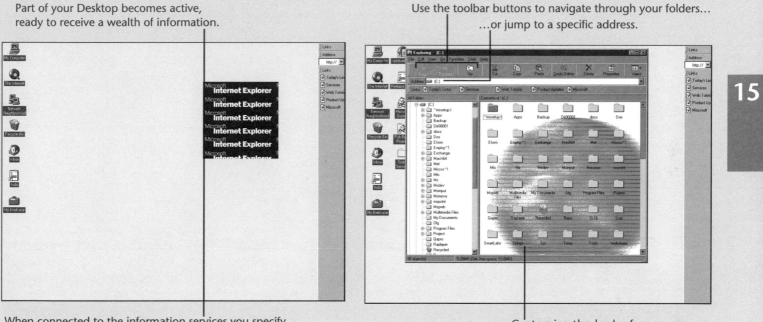

When connected to the information services you specify,
the Active Desktop updates information automatically.

Customize the look of your
windows with a background image.

15

Index

Italicized page numbers refer you to information you'll find in a Tip or a Try This entry.

Enable Indicator On Taskbar
check box (Keyboard
Properties dialog
box), 144
encapsulated objects, 48
enclosures, sending with e-mail,
203. *See also* e-mail
encoded e-mail messages, *203*
encryption (e-mail
messages), *232*
End Task button (Close Program
dialog box), 75
Enter key+Alt key, resizing
windows, 102
Entire Network window, 169
envelope icon (on taskbar), *198*
equipment (hardware), adding
to computer, 164
Eraser tool (Paint), 69, *70*
errors
hard disk, 98
messages
files not found, *51*
Windows Help not
installed, *17*
Esc key+Ctrl key, displaying
taskbar, *119*
events, sounds associated
with, 84
exiting
an MS-DOS program, 108
a non-responsive pro-
gram, 75
Windows, 18
exit (MS-DOS command), 103
Export Registry File command
(Edit menu), 148
Extended Capabilities Port
(ECP) cable, connecting
computers with, *243*
extensions of files, 148
external input devices
(microphones), 82

F

F2 key, editing shortcut
names, *123*
Favorites folder, 251
Favorites list (Internet Explorer),
250–51
Fax Cover Page Editor, 213
fax documents. *See also*
Microsoft Fax
cover pages
creating, 213
information from Address
Book in, *207*
information included
on, *211*
receiving, 214–15
sending, 211, 212
setting up, 210
faxes, network, 184–85
faxes, shared, 182–85
Fax Modem Properties dialog
box, 214
file extensions, 148
File Manager (Windows
version 3), 54, *57*
File menu (Backup window),
92, 95
File menu (Fonts folder), 160
File menu (Paint), 72
File menu (WordMail), *197*
File menu (WordPad)
saving files, *64*, 121
updating embedded object
information, *49*
filenames
finding, *30*
renaming, 103
sorting files by, 24, *25*
symbols used in, 67

files
access to
limited by user
profiles, *121*
on networks, *31*
protecting from, 175
associations, 146–47, 148
backing up, 92–96
compressing for storage, 261
copying
to Briefcase, 230
to different drive, *36*
to floppy disks, 39
to other folders, 37
using MS-DOS com-
mand, 103
using Windows
Explorer, 56
damaged, *98*
defragmenting, 97
deleting
from floppy disks, 58
restoring, *42*
from Windows
Desktop, 128
folders containing, *232*
hiding, 44
information about, 29
managing with Briefcase,
228–30
managing with Windows
Explorer, 56–57
moving, 36, 56
on multiple computers,
228–30
organizing, 27, 36–37, *52*
properties of, 26, 29
protecting from access, 175
read-only, 175
recovering damaged, *98*
saving
to floppy disk, 39
to Windows Desktop, *121*

files, *continued*
searching for, 30–33
in Backup window, *96*
in Windows Explorer, 55
selecting
multiple, *37, 56*
without starting
programs, *11*
sending
via e-mail, 203
via fax, 211
via modem, 222–23
shared, 172–73, *175*
size of
graphics, altering, *51*
searching by, 32
sorting, 24–25
updating Briefcase, 229
file structure. *See also*
directory trees
described, 21
navigating through, 110
file types
associating with programs,
146–47, 148
extensions, 148
hiding, 44
icons for, 149
searching for files by, 32
sorting files by, 24, *25*
system files, 44
used in WordPad, 60, *64*
File Types tab (Options dialog
box), 146
Find command (Tools menu,
Inbox), *205*
Find dialog box (Find submenu),
30, 33
Find dialog box (Windows
Explorer), 55
floppy disks
copying Briefcase files or
folders to, 228–29

Hide MS-DOS File Extensions
For File Types That Are
Registered check box
(Options dialog box), 43
hiding system files, 44
History folder (Internet
Explorer), *251*
Home button (Internet
Explorer), 247
host computers (on networks), 166
HTM files, 149
HyperTerminal, 220–23
hypertext documents, icon
for, 149

I

icons. *See also* Windows
Desktop, icons
arranging, 22, 128
clicking to start programs, 10
customizing
changing, 264
resizing, 124
spacing between, 125
default size, *125*
dragging and dropping,
22, 104
for file types, 149
moving, 22
Image menu (Paint), 72
images. *See* graphics images
Inbox. *See also* e-mail; WordMail
default settings, 194
delivery options, 197
dialing phone numbers from
Address Book, *225*
finding messages in, *205*
folder system, 204–5
font settings, 194
formatting text in, *197,* 200

Inbox, *continued*
notification of new
e-mail, 198
profiles for, *185*
requirements for use, 194
sending faxes and e-mail
from same
message, 212
services accessed
through, 194
setting up, 194–95
on shared computers, *233*
spelling checker, 195
using with online
services, 208–9
viewing logon screens for
services, *239*
views in, *199*
Inbox messages
addressing, 196
attaching files to, 203
encoded, *203*
forwarding, 202
moving between folders, 204
reading, 198–99, *202*
receiving from remote
location, 235
replying to, 200–201
sending, 196–97
sending faxes and e-mail
from same
message, 212
unread, *199*
Inbox Setup Wizard
CompuServe settings, 209
creating new profiles using,
184, 238–39
fax settings, 184
Inbox settings, 194
Include Subfolders check box
(Browse button, Find
dialog box), 30
Index tab (Help Topics dialog
box), 16, 276

information
about files and folders, 29
from Address Book
in mail-merged
documents, *207*
on fax cover pages, *211*
linking to, 50–51
losing after closing
programs, *75*
MS-DOS, 43
storing on floppy
disks, 38–39
Insert File button (Inbox), 203
Insert File command (Edit
menu, Sound
Recorder), 83
Insert File dialog box, 203
Insert menu (WordPad), 62, 63
Insert Object dialog box, 62
Installation Wizard, 158
installing programs, 158
Install New Font command (File
menu, Fonts folder), 160
Install/Uninstall tab
(Add/Remove Programs
Properties dialog box),
158, 159
IntelliMouse, 268–70. *See
also* mouse
IntelliPoint 2.0 software,
137, 259
Internet. *See also* e-mail;
Internet Relay Chat;
intranets; newsgroups
(Internet); World
Wide Web
connecting to computers
on, 220–21
described, 245
intranets compared
with, 245
Windows 95 support on,
280–86, 288

Internet Explorer
blocking access to certain
sites, *247*
described, 245
going to sites
by moving back or
forward, 247
by searching for
topics, 247
by typing address, 246
by using Favorites
list, 250
start page, setting, *247,* 248
toolbar options, 246, 247
Internet Explorer Startup Kit
components of, *189*
described, 245
Internet Mail, using, 258. *See
also* e-mail
Internet News window, 254–55.
See also Microsoft Internet
Mail And News
Internet Relay Chat, 252–53
Internet service providers (ISPs),
208–9, 258
Internet Shortcut tab (Favorites
folder), 251
intranets, 245, 246–47, 248, 251
item properties, displaying from
Toolbar, 26

K

Keyboard Properties dialog
box, 144
keyboards
customizing, 117
layout, 144
mouse compared with, 14
non-English, 144
Knowledge Base, 284–85. *See
also* Internet

program windows. *See also*
    Windows; *names of*
    specific components
closing, 13, *23*
components of, 6–7
customizing, 23, *109*
described, 47
for disk drives, 22
document windows
        compared with, 47
for folders, 28
managing, 12–13
maximized, 12
minimized, 6, 12
moving, 12, 266
opening, 102
organizing, 28
overlapping, 46
resizing, 12–13, 102
resizing panes (Windows
        Explorer), 59
restored, 12
scrolling with Intelli-
        Mouse, 269
switching between, *22*, 46
using a single window, 28
prompt (MS-DOS com-
    mand), 103
prompts
    changing, 103
    MS-DOS, 104–5
properties, 29
Properties command (File
    menu, WordMail), *197*
Properties command (folder
    shortcut menu), 109
Properties command (My
    Computer shortcut
    menu), *39*
Properties command (printer
    shortcut menu), 180
Properties command (Recycle
    Bin shortcut menu), 145

Properties command (taskbar
    shortcut menu), 119, 152
Properties command (Windows
    Desktop shortcut menu),
    122, 129
Properties dialog box, 126
Properties dialog box (MS-DOS–
    based programs), 109
protecting. *See also* passwords
    computer access, 131
    documents against
        formatting, *67*
    files on networks, 175
    folders on networks, 174
    system files, 44
protocols for connecting
    computers, *243*
PST files, in Inbox, 232, 233

Q

question mark (?), used in
    filenames, 67
Quick (Erase) option (Format
    dialog box), 38
Quick View, 73
quitting
    a non-responsive pro-
        gram, 108
    Windows, 18

R

read-only files, 175
Read-Only list of users, 176
Read-Only passwords, 174
Read tab (Options dialog box,
    Inbox), 200
receiving e-mail. *See* e-mail
Record button (Sound
    Recorder), 83

Recycle Bin
    described, 42
    reducing size of, 145
    restoring items from, 35, 42
    sending
        folders to, 35
        items from Windows
            Explorer to, 58
        shortcuts to, 41
    shortcut menu, 15
    viewing contents, *145*
Recycle Bin Properties dialog
    box, 145
Regional Settings Properties
    dialog box, 140
RegEdit program, 148
registry, 148
Remote Configuration tab
    (Microsoft Mail dialog
    box), 234
remote connections
    for e-mail, 232–35
    to networks, 240–41
    preparing modem for, 237
    scheduling, 236
    setup locations, 237
    setup profiles, 238–39
    to terminal, 220–21
Remote Session tab (Microsoft
    Mail dialog box), 234
rename (MS-DOS com-
    mand), 103
renaming
    files, 103
    folders, 35
Replace command (Edit menu,
    WordPad), *65*
Reply To All button (Inbox), 201
Reply To Sender button
    (Inbox), 201
Resize mouse pointer, 13. *See*
    also mouse pointers

resizing
    fonts under icons, 129
    graphics images in WordPad,
        63, 69
    handles for, 63
    icons, 124, *125*
    taskbar, 118, *119*
    window panes (Windows
        Explorer), 59˙
    windows, 12–13, 102
    Windows Desktop, 129
restarting computer, 111
Restart The Computer In
    MS-DOS Mode option
    (Shut Down Windows
    dialog box), 111
Restart The Computer option
    (Shut Down Windows
    dialog box), 117
Restore button
    resizing windows, 12
    returning windows to tiled
        position, *46*
Restore command, 42
restoring items from Recycle
    Bin, 35, 42
retrieving backed-up files, 96
Rich Text Format (RTF) files in
    WordPad, 60, 64
right angle bracket (>), used in
    filenames, 67
right-clicking. *See also* clicking
    (mouse); shortcut menus
    copying files or folders, 39
    described, 14
    opening shortcut menus, 15
    viewing documents, 73
RS-232 null-modem cable,
    connecting computers
    with, *243*
RTF files (Rich Text Format) in
    WordPad, 60, 64
Ruler command (View menu,
    WordPad), 61

Jerry Joyce has had a long-standing relationship with Microsoft: he was the technical editor on 23 books published by Microsoft Press, and he has written manuals, help files, and specifications for numerous Microsoft products. You might also find him prowling around online bulletin boards and news groups, answering questions about getting work done with various software products. Jerry's alter ego is that of a marine biologist; he has conducted research from the Arctic to the Antarctic and has published 18 scientific papers on marine-mammal and fisheries issues. In his spare time he enjoys traveling, birding, and disappearing into the mountains.

Marianne Moon has worked in the publishing world for many years as proofreader, editor, and writer—sometimes all three simultaneously. She has been editing and proofreading Microsoft Press books since 1984 and has written and edited documentation for Microsoft products such as Flight Simulator, Golf, Publisher, the Microsoft Mouse, and Greetings Workshop. In another life, she was chief cook and bottlewasher for her own catering service and wrote cooking columns for several newspapers. When she's not chained to her computer, she likes gardening, cooking, traveling, writing poetry, and knitting sweaters for tiny dogs.

Marianne and **Jerry** own and operate **Moon Joyce Resources**, a small consulting company. They've had a 15-year working relationship and have been married for the last 5 years.

The manuscript for this book was prepared and submitted to Microsoft Press in electronic form. Text files were prepared using Microsoft Word 7.0 for Windows. Pages were composed using QuarkXPress 3.32 for the Power Macintosh, with text in ITC Stone Serif and ITC Stone Sans and display type in ITC Stone Sans Semibold. Composed pages were delivered to the printer as electronic prepress files.

Cover Design and Illustration
Tim Girvin Design
Gregory Erickson

Interior Graphic Designers
designlab
Kim Eggleston

Interior Graphic Artist and Illustrator
s.bishop.design

Typographers
Blue Fescue Typography & Design
Kari Becker Design

Proofreader
Alice Copp Smith

Indexer
Bero-West Indexing Services

Things are looking up!

Here's the remarkable, *visual* way to quickly find answers about the powerfully integrated features of the Microsoft® Office 97 applications. Microsoft Press® *At a Glance* books let you focus on particular tasks and show you with clear, numbered steps the easiest way to get them done right now.

Microsoft Press® products are available worldwide wherever quality computer books are sold. For more information, contact your book retailer, computer reseller, or local Microsoft Sales Office.

To locate your nearest source for Microsoft Press products, reach us at www.microsoft.com/mspress/, or call 1-800-MSPRESS in the U.S. (in Canada: 1-800-667-1115 or 416-293-8464).

To order Microsoft Press products, call 1-800-MSPRESS in the U.S. (in Canada: 1-800-667-1115 or 416-293-8464).

Prices and availability dates are subject to change.

Microsoft® Excel 97 At a Glance
Perspection, Inc.
U.S.A.   **$16.95**   ($22.95 Canada)
ISBN 1-57231-367-6

Microsoft® Word 97 At a Glance
Jerry Joyce and Marianne Moon
U.S.A.   **$16.95**   ($22.95 Canada)
ISBN 1-57231-366-8

Microsoft® PowerPoint® 97 At a Glance
Perspection, Inc.
U.S.A.   **$16.95**   ($22.95 Canada)
ISBN 1-57231-368-4

Microsoft® Access 97 At a Glance
Perspection, Inc.
U.S.A.   **$16.95**   ($22.95 Canada)
ISBN 1-57231-369-2

Microsoft® Office 97 At a Glance
Perspection, Inc.
U.S.A.   **$16.95**   ($22.95 Canada)
ISBN 1-57231-365-X

Microsoft® Windows® 95 At a Glance
Jerry Joyce and Marianne Moon
U.S.A.   **$16.95**   ($22.95 Canada)
ISBN 1-57231-370-6

Microsoft®*Press*

Get quick, easy answers— anywhere!

Microsoft Press® Field Guides are a quick, accurate source of information about Microsoft® Office 97 applications. In no time, you'll have the lay of the land, identify toolbar buttons and commands, stay safely out of danger, and have all the tools you need for survival!

Microsoft® Excel 97 Field Guide
Stephen L. Nelson
U.S.A. $9.95 ($12.95 Canada)
ISBN 1-57231-326-9

Microsoft® Word 97 Field Guide
Stephen L. Nelson
U.S.A. $9.95 ($12.95 Canada)
ISBN 1-57231-325-0

Microsoft® PowerPoint® 97 Field Guide
Stephen L. Nelson
U.S.A. $9.95 ($12.95 Canada)
ISBN 1-57231-327-7

Microsoft® Outlook™ 97 Field Guide
Stephen L. Nelson
U.S.A. $9.99 ($12.99 Canada)
ISBN 1-57231-383-8

Microsoft® Access 97 Field Guide
Stephen L. Nelson
U.S.A. $9.95 ($12.95 Canada)
ISBN 1-57231-328-5

Microsoft Press® products are available worldwide wherever quality computer books are sold. For more information, contact your book retailer, computer reseller, or local Microsoft Sales Office.

To locate your nearest source for Microsoft Press products, reach us at www.microsoft.com/mspress/, or call 1-800-MSPRESS in the U.S. (in Canada: 1-800-667-1115 or 416-293-8464).

To order Microsoft Press products, call 1-800-MSPRESS in the U.S. (in Canada: 1-800-667-1115 or 416-293-8464).

Prices and availability dates are subject to change.

Keep things running smoothly around the Office.

These are *the* answer books for business users of Microsoft® Office 97 applications. They are packed with everything from quick, clear instructions for new users to comprehensive answers for power users. The Microsoft Press® *Running* series features authoritative handbooks you'll keep by your computer and use every day.

Running Microsoft® Excel 97
Mark Dodge, Chris Kinata, and Craig Stinson
U.S.A. **$39.95** ($53.95 Canada)
ISBN 1-57231-321-8

Running Microsoft® Office 97
Michael Halvorson and Michael Young
U.S.A. **$39.95** ($53.95 Canada)
ISBN 1-57231-322-6

Running Microsoft® Word 97
Russell Borland
U.S.A. **$39.95** ($53.95 Canada)
ISBN 1-57231-320-X

Running Microsoft® PowerPoint® 97
Stephen W. Sagman
U.S.A. **$29.95** ($39.95 Canada)
ISBN 1-57231-324-2

Running Microsoft® Access 97
John Viescas
U.S.A. **$39.95** ($53.95 Canada)
ISBN 1-57231-323-4

Microsoft® *Press*

Take productivity in stride.

Microsoft Press® *Step by Step* books provide quick and easy self-paced training that will help you learn to use the powerful word processor, spreadsheet, database, desktop information manager, and presentation applications of Microsoft Office 97, both individually and together. Prepared by the professional trainers at Catapult, Inc., and Perspection, Inc., these books present easy-to-follow lessons with clear objectives, real-world business examples, and numerous screen shots and illustrations. Each book contains approximately eight hours of instruction. Put Microsoft's Office 97 applications to work today, *Step by Step*.

Microsoft Press® products are available worldwide wherever quality computer books are sold. For more information, contact your book retailer, computer reseller, or local Microsoft Sales Office.

To locate your nearest source for Microsoft Press products, reach us at www.microsoft.com/mspress/, or call 1-800-MSPRESS in the U.S. (in Canada: 1-800-667-1115 or 416-293-8464).

To order Microsoft Press products, call 1-800-MSPRESS in the U.S. (in Canada: 1-800-667-1115 or 416-293-8464).

Prices and availability dates are subject to change.

Microsoft® Excel 97 Step by Step
U.S.A. $29.95   ($39.95 Canada)
ISBN 1-57231-314-5

Microsoft® Word 97 Step by Step
U.S.A. $29.95   ($39.95 Canada)
ISBN 1-57231-313-7

Microsoft® PowerPoint® 97
 Step by Step
U.S.A. $29.95   ($39.95 Canada)
ISBN 1-57231-315-3

Microsoft® Outlook™ 97 Step by Step
U.S.A. $29.99   ($39.99 Canada)
ISBN 1-57231-382-X

Microsoft® Access 97 Step by Step
U.S.A. $29.95   ($39.95 Canada)
ISBN 1-57231-316-1

Microsoft® Office 97 Integration
 Step by Step
U.S.A. $29.95   ($39.95 Canada)
ISBN 1-57231-317-X

Microsoft Press